APPLAUSE for PRODIGAL SONG

"Jim Robinson has given us a rare gift: A compelling story, told with vivid detail and eloquent drama. His honesty allows us to find ourselves not only in the memories of heartache, but also in his moments of triumph. His journey from despair to joy can encourage us all."

— Timothy Jones, author of *Awake My Soul,*
The Art Of Prayer, and *Workday Prayers*

Highest Rating (5 Stars): "Prodigal Song ... traces the story of this man's life through the nightmares of alcoholism and drug addiction ... yet something called to him and showed him another path. Postulating the idea that childhood memories could be messengers of spiritual healing, it follows Robinson's revelation of God's whispers ... and his long journey back to life from the depths of despair. A moving and life-affirming portrayal, *Prodigal Song* is spiritually rewarding and reader inspiring."

— *Midwest Book Review*

"Beautifully written ... the language is captivating, the transparency both staggering and refreshing. Jim Robinson has authored a book that reaches out to everyone who has ever felt the pain of being lost and the joy of being found. Like his music, this story strikes a beautiful chord."

— Ron Doyle, Vice-President,
Christian Leadership Concepts, Inc

"Highest rating — a Must Read! This story touched me more than any other story has touched me for a number of years. Robinson writes eloquently of his boyhood, and draws you back into memories that he believes are messages from God. You may find some memories similar to your own when reading Robinson's story. Has God been leaving messages for you?"

— *BookReview.com*

"With startling clarity and unbridled honesty, Robinson takes the reader not only on a journey through his life, but on a trail of psychological torture, speaking with the rare gift of one who has been there and can recount the trip. Ultimately, though, Robinson's message is one of healing, and this is what bears the force behind this memoir. Read *Prodigal Song* for the story. But give this book to a friend in need. And after the last chapter, you'll know who needs it — because you will have already met him in these pages."

— Tom Mayer, Editor, *The Daily Southerner*

"The talent for writing is clear from the first page ... Robinson's rich, vivid language makes this remarkable story come to life in a fresh way."
— *The Editor's Word*

"Robinson shows the reluctant grownup in each of us what we perhaps have always suspected — that in the innocent world of childhood, *everything matters*. The themes of life and loss, abandonment and addiction, family and faith, are explored in remarkable poetic prose. *Prodigal Song* is more than a memoir of recovery; it reveals the inner longings of the wounded child in everyone, bringing us face to face with the suffering of spiritual separation that only grace can heal."
— Mike S. O'Neil, LADAC, NCAC 1, author of *Power To Choose, The Church As A Healing Community,* and *Boundary Power*

Highest Rating (5 Stars): "Robinson paints images as lyrical and beautiful and moving and compelling as the songs he writes and sings. His recollections of the good childhood memories in small-town Middle Tennessee are treasured nuggets to savor. His snapshots of the bad times form like dark clouds in the distance. The unfolding of his self-destructive path through adolescence and young adulthood is as stark and gripping as his recovery is inspiring. Jim's story is unique. Yet it is ultimately my story and your story. That's what draws you in. It is a story of love and hate, joy and anger, fear and bravery, despair and hope, evil and good, destruction and salvation. And good, through salvation, is winning. That's what makes it so important."
— William Bowlby, *WordofMouth/bookreporter.com*

"*Prodigal Song* is a terrific book. The sense of immediacy Robinson is able to portray is astounding. A wonderfully-written, inspiring story."
— Andrew Corbin, Editor, *Doubleday Religion*

"This incredible book pulled me into reliving Robinson's story with a compelling force I did not anticipate. His transparency and vivid telling allowed me to feel not only the despair but also the hope of clean, wholesome, fulfilling and authentic living on the road through and beyond addiction. A powerful book of hope for those struggling with or loving those with seemingly invincible demons. *Prodigal Song* unveils the sunrise after the darkest night!"
— Dan Miller, Life Coach and Author of
48 Days To The Work You Love

ProdigalSong

A MEMOIR

James Eugene Robinson

Published by
Good Apple Press
PO Box 33
Franklin, TN 37065

In cooperation with
SonLight Publishing, Inc.
2711 Murfreesboro Road, Suite 105
Antioch, TN 37013

Cover Photography
Z. Bryan Haislip © 2000

Design and layout
1106 Design   *www.1106design.com*

Library of Congress Control Number:
2003094012

Soft cover: ISBN 0-9742248-0-4
Hard cover: ISBN 0-9742248-1-2

Printed in the United States of America
Second Printing

FOR MY SISTERS,
JOETTE AND JENNIFER.
AND FOR DAD.

contents

O Lord! How joyful
and happy must they be,
who, when they come to
consider their own selves,
find in themselves nothing
remarkable whatever.

—*THOMAS MERTON*

I yam what I yam.
And that's all that I yam.

—*POPEYE THE SAILOR MAN*

O nce, in a place and time that now seems near enough to touch and yet just beyond my reach, finding myself caught between the dreams of a boy and the desires of a man, I ran away from Home. This is the story of how I lost myself, and found a Friend.

I'm not really sure how I became lost in the first place. And I'm even more confused about how I managed to stumble out of the storm and end up back where I started, on His doorstep, alive and breathing again. But somehow, somewhere along the line, the person I had always assumed myself to be fell away like an ill-fitting costume, and I discovered inside my skin a stranger, bloodied and dazed like some doe-eyed amnesia victim following a near-fatal accident. From that moment on, I've had to re-learn my life—and perhaps even some purpose for it—one awkward day at a time. It's not easy, accepting something as precious as Grace.

My journey back to faith has been a dangerous one. As with all long journeys, the scenery has at times been less than pretty. And so, although I now see that God has been writing this book inside my heart from the very beginning, the thought of suddenly setting it free to be shared with others fills me with fear. Even after all this time, I feel uncomfortable revealing certain truths about myself; a distant part of me wants to keep my secrets very secret, so that they stand a better chance of destroying me. Most of my life I have too often listened to those voices in my head, the old ones, the ones that have been repeating the same messages for as long as I can remember: *You are not worthy. You're a fraud. No one will love you if they discover who you really are.* Even now, listening, I am afraid. Afraid of a truth I would rather pretend never happened and have never dared share. Afraid of a past about which I have prayed my children might never learn. Maybe—I think—if I hide from it long enough, if I shut my eyes tight enough, maybe it will never have been.

Professionals who work in the field of chemical dependency would quickly identify me as a classic example of the "egomaniac with an inferiority complex." So here I am now with some time in recovery, refereeing a daily battle between the still-struggling part of me that constantly craves attention, and another part that desperately dreads drawing any more notice to myself. Half of me has always fully expected to be famous. And yet, I'm often terribly lonely and afraid, desperately seeking approval, hopelessly hoping that someone might find something within me worth loving. It's a vicious cycle, this all-or-nothing, warp-speed or dead-stop, top-of-the-heap or bottom-of-the-barrel kind of living. So these days I've had to learn to reach out for help, and tell a few trusted people the truth about myself, at least as much truth as I can discern. When I do, I find that I'm able to stay marginally sane.

Over time, though, God keeps pushing. He wants me to dig deeper, I think, and look harder, and stop pretending the healing is complete. Perhaps He longs for each of us to pause on the pathways of our past, and listen for the lyrical messages hidden in our history. It's how we unlock the mystery of our memories—taking a hard, long look at our lives, staring our wounds right in the eye, without blinking, until we find ourselves face to face with Him. We resist, of course, for as long as we're willing to put up with the lingering pain. But eventually the Truth will just literally beat the living hell out of us, if we're willing. And we can't keep our backs turned on Heaven forever.

The Father has remained at my side no matter how frantically I've run in the other direction. And He has been whispering all along, while I made as much useless noise and clatter as possible to cover up the sound of His voice. Little by little, I'm beginning to understand some small part of what He is saying to me, and it's something like this: *You are not what you think you are. You are mine, and you have always been mine, so stop trying to impress me. You can stop all of your ranting and raving, because I am not listening to that. It's time for me to show you some things, and I need you to pay attention. All you have to do is take my hand, and trust. I'll lead you Home.*

So I write. I go back there, all these many memories later, and look for the things God would have me never forget. This is not a book about alcoholism or mental illness or depression, though I have inhabited those worlds. Instead, this is simply a story about remembering, and forgetting, and how God wondrously weaves both together into something that ultimately makes some sense of our lives, if we'll only look and listen. It's about becoming a child again—breathlessly peering around the long-hidden corners, summoning from a place of courage far beyond ourselves the willingness to finally step out and face our fear—and there, in the rebirth of our vulnerability, to dangerously discover the meaning of our dreams.

Though the still-frightened part of me cannot imagine why anyone would be in the least interested in turning through the pages of this scrapbook of my life, here it is just the same: brought out of the cellar, dusted off and spread on the altar—a sacrifice offered up somewhat selfishly, for my own cleansing, in hopes of dragging my secrets out from under the rock of what I once was into the light of who He so lovingly desires me to become.

Since God in His wisdom has decided to both deny and spare me the inevitable embarrassment of superstardom, this will not be the memoir of a famous person. I'm a songwriter, but this is no insider's look at the music business. I'm a trained counselor, too, and although my own family's dysfunction plays an important role in the early part of this story, you won't find much here in the way of therapeutic psychobabble. Ultimately, we're the same, you and I, and in a way this is a story about each of us, about our brokenness, our humanness. All of us have wounds. My story is more colorful than some, and less so than others; it is more tragic than many, yet less tragic than a great many more. All I really know for sure is this: My night was black enough, and the desire for death strong enough, that I can now look into the faces of pain I work with almost daily and see myself there, clearly. I have come alongside the kind of despair that makes suicide seem a very reasonable path to relief. I know, as so many of us do, what it means to hide from Him... the leper in each of us covering our sores with a dirty shawl, ducking into the nearest cave, vainly trying to seal his or her own worst fate—to never be touched or loved again.

This is a true story, at least as true as I can remember it to be, and I have reluctantly come to believe that mine—like the stories each of us carries through our lives—is one worth telling. As in all remembering, this painting is both portrait and pentimento, the truth slowly revealed only through the meticulous removal of many layers. Spoken in the native language of a man reunited with a childhood Companion, this is a faint yet familiar tale of fresh meadows still to be run through, and of shattered dreams and tears of healing in the arms of a long lost Best Friend. It's the story of a modern-day prodigal son, and the singing again of a song from long ago thought forever lost. It is a soul-song, and each of us, if we concentrate, knows all the words by heart.

I hope some will see through the eyes of my journey a version of their own, and learn that while they may have felt forever lonely they have never been truly alone. Perhaps a few others will find something here that might stir in them a curiosity about the messages and meaning within their own memories, and cause them to lean their child's ear a bit closer to Christ's lips. Because, when all is said and done, we have a choice of what we listen for... and what we dream.

≈ *Part One* ≈
dreaming

At that time the disciples
came to Jesus, saying,
"Who then is greatest
in the kingdom of heaven?"
And He called a child to Himself
and set him before them,
and said, "Truly I say to you,
unless you are converted
and become like children,
you shall not enter
the kingdom of heaven."
— *MATTHEW 18: 1–3*

———————

But it isn't Easy...
because Poetry and Hums
aren't things which you get,
they're things which get YOU.
And all you can do is to go
where they can find you.
— *WINNIE THE POOH*

the rope swing

When I was a little boy I had a rope swing. The rope hung from the branch of a giant oak tree that stood in the woods near my house. My father had somehow tied one end of this braided yellow nylon rope to a huge, high branch. From where I stood—way down there on the earth, looking up—the knot holding aloft my innocent hopes appeared to be thousands of feet in the air, small and very far away. And there, in the cool, safe shade of my childhood, I flew fearlessly through the wind, like Tarzan.

Although the knot up there in the sky rested nearly out of my sight, I knew that my father had tied it, and I never worried that it might break. And as far as I can remember, it never did, my yellow rope still lifelessly hanging there long after I thought I'd grown up too much to use it. I was very proud of my father. He was tall and handsome and funny and smart and brave, and if he said the swing was safe, that was good enough for me. But one day, something happened. One day I flew too fast or too high or too recklessly, and I fell. Under my swing lay mostly bare dirt and exposed roots and some of the ever-present white gravel that made up the hills of my small hometown. As I fell, I caught myself with the palms of my hands, or tried to, and slid painfully for several feet. The skin of my hands and chin was scraped away, and the bleeding, though it looked worse than it was, made my heart leap inside my chest. All this happened in a flash of a moment, and in that moment I did the most natural thing in the world. I prayed—"Oh God, please save me!"—or something like that, and I thought it more than said it, though it was a shout from my soul that God couldn't help hearing. And then, I heard something. I heard—*felt*—a voice, and the voice gave me an instant peace. I knew, completely and beyond all doubt, that I was not alone. And the Voice said, in a very huge yet very wordless way, something like this: *I'm right here. I've been here all along. You're safe now.*

The fall itself turned out to be no big deal. It flashed by noisily, a little blood and a mouth full of dirt, without any real injury. But for some reason the experience stands out with such clarity that I can still feel the tingling of it in my palms. The memory has lived in my mind almost daily for forty years, clear and unchanging. I have dreamed it again and again...this hidden but not-quite-lost part of me, a mystical moment in time caught between my head and heart, an unopened hand holding some sort of essential truth, some meaning. It's almost as though Someone, very patiently and for a very long time now, has been trying to tell me something.

Strange, the things we remember, and the things we forget. Perhaps the truth is that we choose which memories we will discard and which we will embrace, or maybe an even deeper truth is that God chooses for us, but either way it seems deeply mysterious. Of all the many days and nights and thoughts in a lifetime, all the hours of our lives spent playing, sleeping, dreaming, loving, crying, laughing...it appears that most of them are lost, while other small and seemingly insignificant events stay with us forever—those flashes in our heads, clear as morning, sharp and tingling as new spring grass on baby-bare feet, memories that seem to have always been a part of us, disjointed, timeless, coming at us in no particular order, meaningless to anyone else and often to ourselves...rope swings and lost turtles and unexplained tears, sweet caresses and red-faced anger, bread-and-butter pickles, shining eyes and sunken eyes, the rhythmic rasp of a million unseen crickets, the feel of wildflowers between our fingers and tadpoles between our toes, shiny black guitars and thunderstorms, fresh cherry tomatoes and thick, heavy quilts...boundless joy and hopeless tears.

I'm looking through a box of pictures. Finally. I've had the box for years. They represent decades of photographs, and after all the time since they were taken had passed, old lives finished and new ones started, families disintegrated and marriages ended and houses sold, somehow they had found their way to Dickie's basement, back in my hometown.

"I've got lots of y'alls pictures down there," he always said, every time I'd visit. Divorced from my older sister for years now, Dickie is still family to me, to all of us, still living in the house where the two of them had raised their three children. "I don't know if you want any of them or not," he'd say, and I would stall and put it off a little longer. And even after finally talking myself into rummaging through them one day and filling up a box to take home, I hadn't looked at them too hard or for too long.

I'll get around to it some time. Some other time. Frame them, hang them on a wall, maybe create a family photo gallery in the hallway of my new house. But it never happened.

A year earlier, Dickie had discovered some old 16mm reels down there, too. Out of curiosity as much as anything else, I'd paid to have them transferred to videotape; for some reason these 15-minute "vacation movies" weren't quite as daunting as the photos. But there wasn't much to see, really. The faded, jerky images only taunted me, bittersweet, incomplete. There was no sound, of course, so everyone appeared mute and trapped back there, my young parents mugging and posing, their mouths open in the silent laughter of a less than convincing pantomime. The camera only rolled for the happy times, capturing barely a glimpse of who we were. I needed to look at them. But they couldn't take me any further.

So now I'm writing. Older, a little slower and more reflective, finally letting the thoughts and words that have rattled and banged around inside my head all this time spill out, trying to make some sense out of them. *Trying to remember.* And I thought the old photographs might help me see some things. So out they come—blowing off the dust, smiling, wincing, crying. Seeing things I'd forgotten and yet somehow never stopped remembering, really, in some never quite grown-up place within. Like the way my father looked when he was in his twenties, chiseled and fearless, or my mother's face, smiling, bright, full of promise. Or how small my two sisters and I once were, and how incredibly blue the sky looked back then, even in a faded old Polaroid.

Now, at last. Outside the rain falls on a dull-gray day in late autumn, and I'm the only one home. It's time. After all that has happened, after so many years. In a way it seems absurd, as though I've suddenly found myself in some maudlin movie. But something in me knows. So I sit on the floor surrounded by this pile of snapshots, feeling sentimental and strangely fearful, wondering what took me so long, wondering if I can take it much longer...

Jimmy, Crawling (Funny!)
I remember this—crawling on the top of my head.
I really do. And here's a photograph of me doing

it (is that why I remember?). As a baby I would put the top of my head on the floor and crawl on all fours, pushing my bald scalp across the rug. I can feel the sensation still, the warmth of the friction, a calming thing, maybe. "Nobody remembers things from when they were that young," my big sister laughs. But I can...

Out of all that we might remember, why these brief bursts of things, the tastes and smells and visions of things long past but never buried, things that come to us from then into now, unexpectedly tugging us loose from whatever false reality we've recently grown accustomed to. One moment standing importantly in our grown-up suits and ties living our grown-up reasonable lives, then suddenly leaning against a wall in the middle of the day, smiling stupidly in the middle of a sentence. Or waiting in line at the grocery store, half awake, our minds stuck in some dull everyday thoughtlessness, in the most ordinary places and at the most ordinary of times, without warning and out of nowhere *something* finds us and invades us—these "glimpses of forgotten dreams," as Tennyson called them. Despite ourselves we laugh out loud or pale with longing or cry new tears for old pain, as if we're suddenly sitting in the mud in our diapers, struck fresh in the face with *feeling* again. Why *these* things, when so many other countless days seem less than a blur, gone for good, finished, millions of thoughts and emotions and experiences now nothing more than lost days on a worn out calendar, as if we had shuffled through much of our lives barely conscious.

These pictures. Something draws me, both physically and spiritually. And on this dreary day a vague yet familiar pain relentlessly wraps itself around me, firmly insisting that my past has been a foreshadowing. It has taken all these years, all these prayers, to come here again, back to this place in my soul where once upon a time the road forked, and Happily Ever After turned into something else.

How did I get here? I'm supposed to be the one with all the answers now. People come to see me, and I talk with them about their overpowering sadness, their utter emptiness, because I have felt those things, too. And sometimes I'll draw diagrams on the chalkboard, and explain things about our brains and our souls, and how we become addicted to substances and possessions and behaviors. I try to sound confident, and informative, and most of all hopeful, because I have certainly come to rely on that Hope. But the real truth is, I'm in many ways just as baffled as they are, because even though I've been clean for a while now it's still mostly mysterious as to how or why I became a drunk and a drug addict in the first place, and an even deeper mystery as to how I got better. It's about much more than my genes or my environment, my will or my weakness. Healing has come slowly, and feels far from complete. Again, Someone tugs at my sleeve. *How did I get here?*—I ask. And a voice seems to say—*Follow Me.*

Here, all these years later, perhaps now far enough from the edge of the pit, I sense there must be more answers, still-hidden truths, a semblance of order to these jumbled puzzle pieces God has woven into my life, into each of our lives—turns in the road, close calls, near misses—as if all along, perhaps even before we were born, He has been planting like seed these hidden messages we now find growing in our hearts. A pair of hands hovering over us, creating out of apparent chaos the tapestry of who we were, became, and might still be. A plan. *Everything matters*: these moments, these ceaseless whispers. *They mean something.*

All these pictures. All these years it took to finally get around to them, really *looking* at them, too busy or too frightened to face them. Busy running, each of us, in different ways and to different places, hiding, making new lives and taking new snapshots for new photo albums. And now I approach them, cautiously, as if the time-stained box were an animal lying still on the ground that might suddenly leap at me if I get too close.

I reach in and pull them out, one by one, all out of order…no real time-line, no sense of natural flow, jumping erratically across the years from toddler to teen to ten and back again, aimlessly lurching through the decades in a broken-down time machine.

Many of them have dates scribbled on the back, and maybe a few words. Much of the handwriting seems to be Mom's. And a lot of it looks like Mamaw's…

the things we remember

Jimmy—Sixteen Months
In the pots and pans again, always digging them
out of the bottom drawer of the oven, banging on
them like bongos. I'm looking back over my
shoulder at the camera; baggy diaper, caught in
the act, a huge guilty smile on my face...

I would be the only boy. My father was an only child.
"You're the last of the Robinson men," he'd say to me

when I was young, only half joking. "It's up to you to keep the line going." It was a running gag. And everyone would laugh. I would laugh, too, a little, though I wasn't really sure why, standing there looking up at all those tall people looking down at me, wondering just what kind of responsibility they were placing on my small shoulders.

One early March morning in 1955, a young doctor assisted God and my mother in bringing me into the world. Dr. Ron, just like my dad, had come to the small Tennessee town to begin his new practice. Quiet, beautiful, and full of promise, my little world rested confidently along the banks of the Tennessee River. The Tennessee Valley Authority was building there, flooding land to create what would become part of the Kentucky Lake Reservoir, and some believed—my father among them—that Camden would one day benefit from its location, maybe even become a boom town. Young couples migrated from all over to settle down and raise their families. Rolling, with heavily forested hills and deep, broad valleys, the little place was a haven for fishing and boating, hunting and camping. As county seat, Camden did seem destined for great growth, though at the time it had no stoplight, no movie theater, and no real industry to speak of. But the boom never happened.

Over the last four and a half decades the little town has not really changed much. Today, a highway with an exit off I-40 runs through the east side, leading to a larger town. Along this stretch the usual clutter has grown up where only the weeds used to be, so that now the town has McDonalds and Burger King and Wal-Mart, and—perhaps most disconcerting of all—a traffic light. Otherwise, the place looks pretty much the same as it did when I was a kid.

For a few minutes there, early on that March morning, Dr. Ron really had Dad going. He might not have admitted it to anyone then, but my father confided later that he had been desperately hoping for a boy. I was the second child, the last one they really planned on, I think, and the last chance to "keep the line going." Joette was seven. She had pleaded with God for a baby brother. I think Momma wanted a boy, too. But when Dr. Ron came into the waiting room to give Dad the news, he said, "Everything went fine, Jim. It's a beautiful baby girl." And Dad blinked and stammered, and finally blurted he was just happy everyone was okay. The Doc allowed him to squirm for a minute, then finally let him in on the gag, and much hugging and backslapping ensued. The story was told again and again as I was growing up, in a celebrative tone, as if implying that by nature of my maleness, some disaster had been averted.

They named me James Eugene. The James part was a tradition; my great grandfather had been James Polk, my grandfather James Talmadge, my father James William. Eugene was the name of my mother's father. And so I arrived, albeit scrawny, a little more than six pounds of hope for the lineage. And everyone was very happy.

Jimmy—Twenty Months
Another one of me in diapers. Standing on my tiptoes, giving Momma a kiss. We're in the kitchen—

*she's small and beautiful, wearing a short-sleeve
white blouse, leaning down to me. Our lips are
just about to touch...*

Impressions. That weird warmth of the rug coming
through the top of my scalp. Tiny wildflowers in front of
my bare toes, *real* blue and white and purple washed in
sunlight, spread out beyond my then-horizon, the never-
ending expanse of the back yard. Faces, up-close, bizarre
faces, huge, strange but comforting—the softness of my
mother's, the sandpaper-rough whiskers and horn-
rimmed glasses of my dad's...and the almost angelic eyes
of my grandmother—*"You're our special, special boy. My
little Jim, bright-eyed Jimmy, Jesus loves you so..."*

Jimmy and Suzie
*No date; I'm five, maybe six. It must be summer.
I'm sitting in the green grass, and my collie, Suzie,
is trying to lick my face. My head is thrown back
in laughter, my arms wrapped around her bushy
neck...*

I remember running, finally, though they thought I would
take forever to even learn to walk, my feet flat as pan-
cakes. But once up, like a colt, I tore off, arms spread out
like wings, through summers full of lightning bugs and
church potluck suppers and kick-the-can, boats and
swimming and sunsets peach and purple, the sweet innocent smell of honeysuckle and the heavy, heady perfume
of magnolia blossoms. I would wake to a sunshine-

flooded yellow room, to the sounds of lawn mowers and barking dogs and children laughing, to fresh smells and fresh adventures, and springing out of bed I would run and barely stop running until I was dragged at dusk by my filthy hand to the bathtub. And beside me through this grand and graceful place ran my dog, Suzie.

My eyes worked better back then; the grass was greener, the sky more blue, all of my senses immersed in the essence of childhood. I remember the breathless, electric summer, and the smell of rubber and glue on a new pair of PF Flyers, and how they turned my legs into springs and my leaps into those of gazelles, rocketing through the woods with Suzie at my heels. And I remember what the world looked like from high in a tree...the unexpected autumn falling all around, and the smell of leaves burning, and faded colors soft and soothing, spread gently over the hills like a quilt, the shadows long and gold and the days quickening to darkness...each child desperately holding on to what was left of the light, running through the orange leaves all red-cheeked and runny-nosed, the still and stark heaviness of approaching winter shooting ice through our nostrils and burning like cold fire in our chests...then, a rare winter snow sneaking into town overnight, taking everyone by surprise, laying its eerie, silent-white glow over everything, and stepping out in our rubber boots onto the glimmering surface of an alien, blind-white world, entering the sharp silence of a place so overwhelming it caused us to hold our breaths and close our eyes against the wonder of it all...walking into the woods with my dad to find the perfect cedar

Christmas tree, then bringing it home, triumphantly, the two men returning with treasure from the wild unknown, the women cheering. And always another spring just as promised, and the rebirth of life and color, a new season surging up in me, the fresh sap charging through my veins like a rushing creek after the thaw.

I remember riding on Dad's shoulders, perched proudly there atop his strong, straight back, on which all the weight of my world was supported, my hands on his ears and my head nearly touching the clouds, never more frightened and never so safe—I could see everything from up there. And Sundays after church eating catfish and hush puppies, and Little League and football and the Dairy Dip and the swimming pool at the park, and a naïve sense of my little town being the whole world nestled there in a kind of blissful alone-ness, where the sun and stars and wind and rain and the very passing of time all belonged to me and no one else...an enchanted existence, one continuous dream occasionally broken into tiny remnants of reluctant waking, my sky the only sky, my world the only world, my God the only God.

And the barely audible echo of footsteps as childhood fleets away, the days all pressed together and hurrying past like shimmering glimpses of a dragonfly darting just above the water's surface, humming, hovering, gone...

Dad and I, outside, in the bright sunshine, together. The images are blurred; is this man a friend of my father's? Is this where they live? A construction site? There is a huge trench—at least it looks huge now in

*my mind—with muddy water rushing through it. A
man is working, digging. My dad is talking to him;
they're laughing. The man has his shirt off, his
shoulders and back deeply tanned, the color of milk
chocolate. I'm playing with his son. I can't remember his name. But I can see his face clearly in my
mind—he looks different, his eyes slanted and set
far apart, his face broad. He's wearing glasses with
thick lenses that make his eyes bug out, as though he
is looking at me through a magnifying glass. He
smiles. He's stocky and bow-legged, and he talks
funny. Retarded. That's what I had heard someone
say. I didn't know what it meant. I like him. He
makes me laugh. There is something about him that
attracts me, makes me want to be near him. I like
making him laugh. I want to make him happy. It's
the first time I can remember that feeling—I can't
bear the loneliness I see in him. I understand it, in
some way. No one should be lonely. His dad was
always yelling at him, as if he was really frustrated
and mad with everything he did. I wondered why
he treated him that way. I knew it hurt to have
someone yell at you and call you stupid. The little
boy just keeps smiling.*

*And now we're playing around, giggling. And
then he falls. In an instant he is gone, into the
trench, swept away as I watch, helpless, his head
bobbing, the brown water rushing into his mouth
and choking his screams, turning him upside
down. I watch him move away from me, and I*

can't make a sound. And then there is yelling and a splash and his father has him, pulling, fighting against the water, his own face filled with fear, my dad reaching down, grabbing, slipping, we've got him, we've got him...

And they have him on his stomach, pushing on his back, and his father is yelling and crying at the same time, straddling his son and pumping with both hands and begging him to come back. I watch, wondering if my friend is going away forever, and I feel my arms and legs shaking—terribly afraid of something, afraid to look any more—until finally there is a gagging sound and he's throwing up, white foamy stuff coming out of his nose and mouth. And his father begins to make a strange sound, a moaning and humming sound, like an animal, almost, like laughing and crying mixed together, and then he wraps his son in his arms and sits there in the mud, sunburned face lifted straight to the sky, rocking him like a baby. He does love him, I thought. The little boy is smiling...

I don't know why this image remains burned into my soul, why this scene still inhabits some distant part of me, clear enough to restart the pounding of my heart. It seems to emanate from a place deeper than mere memory, it's pulse more profound, like some encoded message meant just for me. And yet, my father can't remember it at all. It belongs to me, somehow; my mind has given it a place to live, to remain. Perhaps it was my first real taste of fear—

of realizing how quickly laughter can turn to something else. Maybe it's when I saw how fragile we are, and so easily lost.

West View—1960
Little red brick house. Woods behind the back
yard. Three bedrooms. Gravel driveway. Carport.
A ditch between our house and my buddy Doug's,
with a wooden plank laid across it, like a bridge...

Our house stood, small and proud, on West View Avenue. Tons of kids. A whole gang of us, up and down the neighborhood like a pack of dogs, pure energy unleashed, safe and free, with no thoughts of violence or molesters or even dangerous traffic. Our house was right in the middle of all the action, there on the long, sloping road forever filled with bikes.

Always the shortest legs, always the smallest bike— the race would start at the top of the hill, and I'd leap in front, pedaling furiously—then they'd all zoom past me in a flock, pulling away, the baseball cards clothes-pinned to my spokes roaring in frustration. "Hey Squirt!" the bigger kids teased, but I set my jaw, stubborn and tenacious, never giving up or giving in. I might get roughed up playing back yard football, but it made me tough. I held my ground. Coming home routinely battered and bruised, I was careful not to let Mom see how much it really hurt. I wanted desperately to be brave, especially for her sake.

These were good years, and I had good friends, brave backyard partners, fellow explorers. As we grew, changing, so did our bodies, our temperaments, our allegiances. Doug, Shorty, John, Jerry, Kent—blood brothers all, during one season or another. We shared our wonder and innocence as easily as we shared our candy and root beer. I *should* remember them.

But why do I remember Phil? We were never best friends. I don't know why I think of him so often, far more frequently than the others. It's not at all clear why he keeps showing up in my life these days, standing quietly in the corner of my mind, or walking past me on the street, his eyes refusing to meet mine. The many memories of countless days spent with my other buddies can't stir in me the same inner feelings of longing and loneliness as does the shadow of this one dark, shy little boy. I only spent a few brief days with him, during one summer pressed between so many other summers. Why does God keep bringing him to me, asking me to remember?

Phil was the new kid, just moved into the old, somewhat rundown house up our street. I'd seen him that first day, standing in the grown-over back yard with his hands shoved deep into his pockets, shirt-tail out, eyes fixed on the ground. For some reason, at that moment I dedicated myself to becoming Phil's friend.

This would not be easy, though. Phil had a pet chicken. It just sort of hung out in his back yard all day, brainlessly pecking at the grass. Every time I walked up the street to Phil's house, the chicken attacked me. There was an otherworldly quality about this creature; more than once it chased me nearly all the way back to my house, much to the amusement of everyone watching, making me feel silly and small and cowardly. But even this wasn't enough to keep me from my quest. I kept going back.

Phil was strange. I felt drawn to him. He seemed unhappy, and it bothered me that he rarely smiled. I wanted to make him smile. It would keep me awake some nights, this wondering about Phil. I couldn't bear to think of him—of anyone—being lonely.

I invited him to my birthday party.

"I didn't know he was your friend," my mother said.

"Well, he's not exactly," I said. "But no one else pays any attention to him. I think he's *waiting* for a friend." Momma was very pleased with my budding compassion. She explained that Phil's father didn't live with their family anymore, that his mom didn't have a lot of money, and so he might not be able to bring me much of a present. I decided that whatever he brought me, I would try to like it.

On the day of my party, Phil and his mother came to our house, holding a present wrapped in the funny pages of the Sunday newspaper. Phil didn't talk much. I kept watching him from across the room, and even though I was having fun with my friends, I couldn't help feeling sorry for him. It was as though I could sense the very essence of his sadness, and felt attached to it, unable to fully enjoy myself. I kept watching him, searching.

When the time came to open presents, I chose Phil's first. It was a big picture book called "Lad, A Dog"—an inexpensive dime-store book, but nonetheless beautiful to me, especially the full color cover with Lad standing proudly on a hill, the wind making his long collie coat wave like a gold and white banner. I figured Phil must have known I would like it, since I had a collie of my own. I made such a fuss about it, and kept thanking him so profusely, over-reacting, trying desperately to get him to lift his eyes from the floor, that my mother had to eventually steer me away to open the other gifts. Phil never did smile.

I have no idea what ever happened to him. He moved away, before we really had a chance to become friends. I hope he reclaimed whatever childhood had been stolen from him. I hope he had some joy in his life. I'm not sure why I think of him as often as I do, or why his face stays in my mind—dark eyebrows furrowed and frowning, always staring at the ground as if life loomed over him with fists clenched, ready to strike. I wanted to give him something, though I wasn't sure what, this little kid drag-ging his dreams along behind him like a pair of worn-out shoes he didn't want the other kids to see.

If he would just look up. *His eyes...my eyes...*

My little town was a good place, with good people. It did not hurry, moving at its own pace, relaxed, like a good evening walk. A place very much at peace with itself. And in this town, as a boy, before I had dreams of my own, I had *God-Dreams*.

I dreamed I could fly. I had the dream a lot—effort-less, three steps, arms spread, and I would rise up on the wind...somehow aware that it was a dream, and that my flight would be temporary—blissful, finite, as natural as breathing. I also seemed to understand in this sleeping part of me that the dreams were a gift, God-Dreams, something that He knew made me happy, and sent to me often.

I dreamed of being a superhero. I liked comic books. Fantastic Four, The Hulk, X-Men, The Silver Surfer, The Flash. But my favorite was Captain America. My affection for this character had nothing to do with patriotism, or with his uniform or fighting style. Even in the mid-1960's his image seemed a bit dated, and compared to most of the new superheroes in the world he was admittedly plain. He'd been genetically altered in some way, I think, and made into a sort of super soldier; he was bigger and stronger than most men, a real fighting machine. He had a really cool stars-and-stripes uniform and shield, you couldn't deny that. But unlike many of the more modern "mutant" characters, he was basically just a man. He usually got by more on pure tenacity than anything else. He possessed a fighting spirit, it seemed to me, very vulnerable yet indomitable, a guy you could bend but not break, beat up but not beat down, because he just wouldn't quit. He couldn't fly or shoot fire out of his body or transform into some other creature or breathe through gills and live underwater. But he could pursue an opponent until, through what sometimes seemed like sheer willpower, he had achieved victory. He had no super power. But he had staying power. And I think, looking back, that his mortality is what attracted me most. *Because*—I thought—*it's pretty easy to look impressive when you're riding a silver surfboard through space. But it takes a lot of courage to fight evil when you're nothing more than human.*

Papaw and Jimmy—Summer, 1960
Papaw and I had gone fishing. Now we're standing
in his backyard. I'm holding three little bream on a
stringer, on a bright, blue day. We're laughing, my
grandfather and I, both of us missing our front
teeth…

Mamaw stands in the yard, near her rose bushes. Waiting
for me. There, in the clean sunlight, holding an apple, or
perhaps an orange. She would extend it to me like a treasure, like some rare and precious and valuable thing, the
way people who have known hunger and hard times and
sadness often hold things in their hands, comprehending
their true worth. She would place the fruit in my hands as
if bestowing upon me a great gift, which of course it was.
And she would say without speaking—*Here is something*
very special, for someone very special, on this wonderful
day in this wonderful world full of very special things.
And we would celebrate, she and I, the texture and taste
of it, the gift of it.

And then Papaw had taken me fishing. I had never
fished from a boat before.

I'm wearing a straw hat, and Papaw is standing just
a step behind me and to one side, the wide brim of
his Stetson casting a shadow over half his face. He's
motioning to me, encouraging me to hold out the
string wide, to show off my catch…

I have a song. Papaw gave it to me, and to my sisters. He claimed it was an old song from his own childhood, though knowing him it had probably gone through a lot of creative editing and embellishing since it had first been sung to him. He would hold me on his lap, facing him, and his eyes would dance and squish half-closed as he sang out of tune:

> Come waltz me around again Willie
> Around, around, around
> Come waltz me around again Willie
> Around...around...around

That was all of it, all he had, anyway. And it was enough, because when he sang he was always smiling, a nearly toothless smile so wide his eyes squinted shut and his whole face wrinkled. Finishing the song, he'd laugh out loud, a full, gentle, raspy kind of laugh, and we'd applaud and laugh with him. Every time. Again and again, *Come waltz me around again Willie...around, around, around...*

Papaw told the same stories over and over. Usually we were all having lunch after church, the family sitting together, our elbows on Mamaw's white tablecloth. Spread before us were fresh and fabulous things—a platter of fried chicken, yellow squash with onions and black pepper, mashed potatoes, pole beans cooked down with a fat chunk of bacon, red beets in vinegar and sugar, corn bread and homemade blackberry preserves, and "stir-em-up"— our own Benton County Sorghum Molasses ("the finest ever made, anywhere," according to Papaw) mashed with fresh butter and spread thick on hot buttermilk biscuits. There were always plenty of Mamaw's bread-and-butter pickles, and for dessert maybe an apple or peach pie, or—once a year—a sweet-tart gooseberry cobbler, miraculously produced from the scraggly and pitiful little bush in her back yard, which, despite looking quite dead all year round, was always good for one fine cobbler each summer. By the time she laid everything out, very little of her white tablecloth was left showing.

These occasions provided the perfect opportunity for storytelling, because Papaw liked a meal to last a long time; with only four or five good teeth left, he ate slowly and deliberately, somehow successfully devouring any kind of food, even corn on the cob, though it took him a good while to do it. He loved to eat. And after each and every meal, for as long as I can remember, he would say to Mamaw as she scurried around the kitchen, barely taking a bite herself—"Mighty fine, Maw, mighty fine. Best meal you ever cooked." And each and every time, she blushed.

My sisters and I begged for the stories, Mom and Dad rolled their eyes, and Papaw would lean back in his chair and begin: tales of past adventures in his life, amazing things, things from another time and place.

"...and the doctor looked inside, and shook his head again, and said he'd never seen anything like it before in all his years of practicin' medicine," he'd say, closing in on the big finish for the hundredth time, his eyes getting wide. Our eyes would widen, too—"What did he say, Papaw? What did he say?" A brief moment of dramatic silence, honed by years of practice, beautifully timed: *"Born without tonsils! No sign of 'em! Here I was a grown man, and no sign whatsoever that I'd ever had a tonsil in my throat!"*

We gasped.

"...Jimmy had the lucky side," Papaw told everyone. "He caught the only fish in the river. I fished one side of the boat and he fished the other. I didn't get a nibble." And he laughed, and everyone oohed and ahhed and clapped. The little fish, barely bigger than my hand, gleamed and shined on my stringer like a gold and silver necklace in the sunlight. I had never felt so proud...

His mother had been one-quarter Cherokee, or so he claimed, though other than Papaw's unusually high cheek bones the evidence for this appeared at best shaky, and my father never seemed fully convinced. About his parents, Papaw never said much. About his own father, he said nothing at all. His family history remained for the most part a mystery, though he did claim that his grandparents had owned a cabin in the woods of Murray, Kentucky, and that the infamous outlaw Jesse James had once stopped and asked for breakfast.

"He was a polite as he could be," Papaw would say, and then the spark in his eye. "And when he got ready to leave..."—a perfect pause—"...he handed my granddaddy a five dollar *gold piece!*"

Gasps.

Papaw and Jimmy
No date. But it looks to be about the same time as the fishing trip, give or take a year. We're standing in Papaw's garden, the broad green leaves of cucumber and squash up past my knees, the corn and pole beans high over our heads behind us. Papaw has one hand on my shoulder, the other hanging by his side, a cigarette between his fingers. The top of my head comes to his waist...

I admired him. Papaw knew how to exist within the moment, to sit still in the shade of a spreading yard oak, or on the back porch with his feet on a small wooden stool, quiet, restful, moving in a slow waltz with the day rather than rushing against it. He sometimes sat near the edge of his garden, very still—*like a Cherokee Indian, I thought*—hoe between his legs, waiting in ambush for vegetable-eating moles. He could sit like that for half a day. He relished each moment, each taste of food, diligent and deliberate in performing the simplest tasks, like sharpening his knives or polishing his shoes or filling his pipe.

Together, Papaw and I waited out the stark and heavy winters. Though he assured me that the trees were only sleeping, to me they looked dead, their bare and bony arms grasping at the morbid sky. But spring always came. The warmth would spread through the two of us, and together on our knees we'd worship the newborn days, turning up the cold, sleeping soil, offering it to the sun, breathing it in, rolling it in our hands.

Papaw liked keeping things. He let me sit with him at the old wooden desk in his bedroom and examine his treasures. I loved rummaging through that desk. It smelled like *time*. In it were wonderful things, things he had kept forever, since the world was new, things he had been saving to give me when I was "old enough"—horehound candy, Juicy Fruit gum, silver dollars and buffalohead nickels, handkerchiefs with little 'R's Mamaw had sewn into the top corners, toothpicks, his pocket watch, a ball bearing, licorice and paper clips, and pocketknives of every shape and size. These were his possessions, neatly lined up in the musty drawers, worthless, priceless, precious things, manly things that he could only share with me, the next James-in-line.

"Find out who you are," he would say to me, again and again. "And then *be that.*"

Once, after I had been begging for a while, Papaw finally agreed to build a go-kart. I wanted one desperately; I had seen a picture in a magazine, and it was all I could talk about, all I could think about. It became his pet project. We went together to Hall's Hardware Store on the court square, a grown-up place smelling of sawdust and seed and oil and fertilizer, and Papaw bought plywood and brackets and screws and paint.

Back in his workshop—a tiny little shed in the backyard he called "The Little House"—he worked on my racing machine for weeks. I watched as he measured and sawed and sanded for hours on end, his calloused, bigknuckled hands brown and wrinkled as walnuts.

Eventually, it began to look like a real racer, with axles and wheels and an empty place that was to be my driver's seat. Finally, it was done except for painting.

"Mighty fine," Papaw said.

"Mighty fine," said I.

"It'll need a name," he said, taking off his hat and wiping his brow. "Better be thinkin' 'bout a name." Out of the corner of my eye, I watched him, and took my hat off and wiped my brow, too. The two of us stood side by side under the sweltering summer sun, smiling in admiration.

"It looks *fast*," I said breathlessly. "I want to call it The Flash." And so he painted it white, and later in the afternoon he took black paint and put a lightning bolt all the way down the side, then underneath in crude letters: THE FLASH.

"Sun's almost gone," he said, the two of us with our hands on our hips. "Paint oughta be dry tomorrow."

That night, I dreamed of flying through my neighborhood, the envy of everyone.

The next morning, I took my first ride. Down the rough-paved road beside my house, legs stretched out inside its hollow shell, my hands on the steering wheel, gravity the only engine. It shook. The Flash didn't go nearly as fast or as smooth as I had dreamed. It made my teeth rattle. Papaw and my dad stood and watched and laughed as I went down the hill, then came to help me drag it back up.

For some reason, I didn't want to ride again. I don't know why. I refused to get back in. I was disappointed somehow, somewhere deep down, and I didn't want to talk about it. Sullen and silent, I just wanted to go do something else, to get away from it. Papaw and Dad carried it to the house, and I didn't play with it again.

Our house sat at the top of a big, steep, grass-covered hill. In summer, we would race down through the tall brown weeds on flattened cardboard boxes, and during winter if it snowed the entire town seemingly showed up for sledding. This was *my* hill, and from its edge I could view the great expanse of my world.

One day, I realized that my go-kart was missing. For weeks it had sat motionless in our open carport. Usually I walked by it, glancing at it warily, the two of us still inexplicably estranged. But on this day I heard voices, carried up by the breeze to the top of my hill. Following the sound, I crossed through my back yard and peered over the grassy edge down to the field below. I saw several older boys dismantling something.

It was The Flash.

I pulled back, crouching behind a tree, heart thumping. Slowly, I leaned out again, trying to see and not be seen. I couldn't make out details from way up there, but I could see my go-kart, or what was left of it. They had stolen it. They were taking it apart.

The Flash was lost. I couldn't see who these older boys were, couldn't see the expression on their faces. But I could hear their laughter floating up, and I felt they were laughing at *me*. I spied, safe on top of my mountain, sitting now in just the right spot behind my tree, watching them...taking the wheels off, turning it upside down, standing on top like conquering warriors...and then I covered my eyes. There, behind the safe blackness of my palms, I saw myself dashing down the hill, waving a stick above my head like a sword, scattering them, heroically saving my go-kart. It was very real, in my mind. But then, peeking out between my fingers, I forced myself to look at what was truly happening, even though it seemed less real to me than what I saw in my head. I hated them. And I hated myself, biting the inside of my mouth until it bled, the way I always did when upset or afraid. I don't know how long I sat there. After a while, the light began to fade. I wiped my eyes on my sleeve and went inside my house.

In the days that followed, no one came to my rescue. For whatever reason, they chose to let me deal with the problem on my own. If my dad and Papaw had decided this was to be some sort of right of passage, perhaps, an early test of character, then I knew I had failed. I felt like a coward, as if I were letting someone down. I refused to answer any questions, or to even speak of it. It was the last I ever saw of The Flash.

Papaw never said a thing. But he was deeply disappointed. I could see it in his eyes. And at least to some degree I became aware over the next few weeks and months of something connecting and yet separating the three of us, something silently shared between me and my father and his father. When hurt or afraid or filled with feelings of longing or a desire to communicate, we simply stuffed it all away, closing our mouths, our minds, our hearts. We kept quiet, holding it in, pretending not to notice. I don't believe that another word was ever spoken between the three of us about The Flash. It was a sad, silent, unaccountable thing, and we were all afraid to go anywhere near it, ever again.

Jimmy—First Grade Class Picture, 1961
They called me "Squirt." For a while there was some concern that I wasn't growing enough. In elementary school I was by far the smallest boy, and almost all of the girls were bigger than me, too. When we would line up and file into the hall-way for a water break, the teacher always brought along an empty milk crate, and when it was my turn to drink she put the crate down in front of the water fountain for me to stand on. Me and one other little girl. We were the only two who couldn't reach...

Looking up. Looking up at the faces of those I loved. Looking up at the buildings, the pictures on the walls, the clouds, the sky. Looking up towards the top of that oak tree, trying to see where the rope was tied. Looking up after a fall. Always needing to be lifted up in someone's arms to see over the crowd, the parade, the game. Lifted up to see something forbidden, like the time my parents decided it was time to show me death.

Mrs. Belford, a teacher at the elementary school, had died in a car accident. She was dark-haired and beautiful, I thought, and I loved her. And then one morning she wasn't at school, and all of the tall people were strangely quiet and sad. Our substitute teacher couldn't stop crying, and finally the principal sent everyone home.

"We're going to the funeral home to see Mrs. Belford," my mother explained, clipping a fake bowtie onto my shirt collar. She wet a black plastic comb and ran it through my hair. Drops of water ran into my eyes. "She's passed away, honey. She went to sleep last night and never woke up. She's gone to Heaven."

Passed away. Never woke up. What does that mean? How will we see her if she's gone to Heaven?

"We're going to the funeral home to say goodbye," she said, and we went. To this strange and nearly silent place, smelling of stale flowers and perfume and something else I couldn't quite identify but remember still. People were dressed the way they dressed for church. Everyone looked odd, their faces drawn, as if they were all a bit embarrassed and confused.

And then I remember looking up at the big, shiny box. It was dark gray, with golden handles along the sides and on each end. Half of the box was open, and from down there where I stood I could see the inside of a big raised lid lined with lacy white fabric, like something you would see in a baby's crib. I don't remember feeling anything until my father's hands went around and lifted me, and I was looking down into the box.

Mrs. Belford looked very pretty and happy and appeared to be sleeping. But I knew in an instant that she was not there. I could have reached across the space between us and touched her face, but it wouldn't have changed anything. I wasn't at all sure what I *was* seeing, or what any of it meant. I only knew that my heart began to pound and I felt afraid, and I realized that it was her and yet not her, so that in a flash of knowing I understood we were not any of us quite what we seemed to be, that we were all somehow more than our bodies, more than who and what we appeared. I sensed that there was something inside of us that makes us *go*, the way hills make go-karts go, something that could be with us one moment and then suddenly leave our bodies empty and hollow and forever still. I was breathless, frozen for the briefest of instants between life and death, looking down for the very first time on someone I had always looked up to—confused, missing her, not recognizing her, wondering where she had gone...

Tarzan. Captain America. A Down's syndrome boy, drowning, reaching desperately for his father. Even the first tentative look into the face of death.

Perhaps the things that follow us and remain alive within us are gifts, small pieces of Divinity, treasures God puts in our grass-stained back pockets from a long-ago summer, time-jewels meant to be brought out and delicately turned in our hands when it's raining outside and the rest of the world sleeps. Maybe it has little to do with us, really, these fragile, indestructible, unexplainable moments that seem to brush by us like a soft hand against our wondering faces...a mother's hand...God's hand.

Ruth—1959
Looks like one of those Olan Mills studio portraits. Even in this brown, curling photograph, she radiates a calm, almost tangible peace. Her

*head is turned slightly to one side, as if she is look-
ing at someone just out of frame, someone no one
else can see...*

I had mumps, chicken pox, and lots of tonsillitis. And
looking up through the dim fog of my fever it was often
Mamaw's face I saw, poised and floating above me like a
spirit. She sang softly and put cool washcloths on my
forehead. She rubbed Vap-O-Rub on my chest and read
Mother Goose. I lay there on Mamaw's green couch while
she fed me spoonfuls of Cream of Wheat, slowly,
singing...

> *Matthew, Mark, Luke, and John,*
> *Bless the bed that I lie on.*
> *Four angels round my bed;*
> *Two of them stand at my head,*
> *Two of them stand at my feet,*
> *All will watch me while I sleep...*

I stayed with my grandparents a lot. I loved being
with Mamaw and Papaw, safe inside the feel and smell of
their little house—Mamaw's voice, the softness of her
singing, the cool of her quilts, the grace of her hand on my
forehead—*My little Jimmy, Sweet Jesus loves you so...*

Looking up. Lying in bed and looking up at the ceiling,
listening. At some very early point in my life God simply
came up alongside and shouldered His way in. I was tuned-
in to something. Some *One*. I could hear things. Some were
real sounds, the kinds of things everyone can hear, and
some were different, silent sounds, things meant just for

me. I knew God loved me, and He gave me gifts. Every breath felt charged with newness and excitement. He was, without my really being conscious of it, much more real than the world around me. He *was* the world. So that, falling from the rope swing, my calling out His name had been instinctive. On that day, as on so many others, I had felt His *nearness*. I accepted His presence with easy innocence; He was as real as the rope and the gravel and the pain and the taste of the earth. I knew He was near, and I knew He was not Make Believe. And I would always know, even when much later in my life I tried to make believe He wasn't there at all.

Back then, God and I shared, like close friends. I talked to Him all the time, and I knew He could be counted on. When fear threatened, I especially felt Him close by. In the middle of the night, the wind brushing unseen cedar branches against my window, I would whisper things— *Please, God, make me tall, and make me brave*—and always there would come a still peace, and a strong, silent voice.

I'm right here. I've been here all along. You're safe now...

Then, sleep.

Joette, Jennifer, Jimmy—Easter 1962
In the backyard, flowers everywhere, dressed up for church. There is a white swing behind us. The sky is a brilliant blue, the sun shining on our blond heads. Jennifer, born two years after me, stands passively, smiling obediently. I'm holding

what looks like a dead weed, acting silly. Joette
looks like she'd rather be doing something else...

My family was not overtly "religious." My sisters and I
were, like most other kids we knew, dragged along to
church every Sunday, and in our particular case the
church was called "First United Methodist Church." I
always wondered how our church got to be First, and if
there were any Second or Third United Methodist
Churches anywhere. I had never seen any. Anyway, this
was our church, and although we attended regularly, I
have no idea why. I suppose my parents felt it was the cul-
turally correct thing to do, that it was a "good" thing for
the children, and so on. As to my parents' spiritual journey at the time, I know little or nothing. Most of the middle class families in our town went to a church of some
kind, and we went to this one. I don't recall very many
conversations about God or Jesus once we had returned
home, unless somehow the names were being used in an
attempt to instill some sense of guilt or awareness of our
being watched.

"God sees everything," they would tell us, and we
suspected that to be true. "Don't think you can fool *Him*,"
they would add, thereby hoping to assign to us a kind of
celestial baby-sitter. It worked, for the most part. We were
good kids, I think, in a good family. But there was little in
the way of spiritual modeling at the time to account for
my preoccupation with Christ. And yet, something about
Him fascinated me from very early on. The stories I heard
about Him in Sunday School resonated with something

warm and familiar. It was as though my blood flowed with a longing for Him.

And, looking back now, I see the face of someone with whom I shared my first tastes of rich and wordless worship...and feel fresh again the touch of gentle hands, planting seeds of faith deep into my soul.

Jimmy and Jennifer — Mamaw's —
Watson Street — 1962
Standing in front of the white frame house. We must have stayed with them the night before. We're still in our pajamas. Jennifer is holding a white stuffed bunny. My little sister is adorable, round faced and gentle, always quiet, withdrawn, fragile even then. Mamaw has her hands on our shoulders...

She was named Ruth, but we all called her Mamaw. She believed in God and in the scriptures, and she believed in having fun. Beautiful, with creamy-soft skin and penetrating, slate-gray eyes, her laugh came easily and floated through the air like music. She was eighty-nine years old when she died, and not once did she ever cease being a child.

Once, Papaw was furious when Mamaw hurt her ankle. She had decided, on a particularly splendid spring day, to ride a bicycle, something she had not attempted in decades. Sitting in her armchair with an ice pack draped across her foot, she listened quietly as Papaw—who never got very mad very often—chastised her for such foolish behavior.

"You're not a kid anymore," he huffed, leaving the house. The screen door slammed, his footsteps trailed away, and there was silence. Finally, Mamaw looked up at me, sheepishly, and grinned.

"Yes," she whispered. "I *am*."

Mamaw and Papaw, California, 1932
Cool clothes, hard faces, eyes dark in the black
and white photo, faces old beyond their years,
standing by an ancient car on a dirt road. It looks
like orange groves in the background...

They never had much money. When my father was a little boy the three of them experienced times of hungry poverty. Papaw, known to the rest of the world as James Talmadge Robinson, was born in 1895. He was a mostly uneducated roustabout who, following service in the Army during WWI, returned home to Murray, Kentucky and married a girl named Ruth. When the Great Depression came, the family was uprooted, leaving Papaw to search for whatever work he could find. One of his more colorful jobs was as a "test driver" for the Firestone Company, piloting rickety old Fords across the California desert to determine the durability of new tires. As a kid, this always sounded to me like the perfect way to make a living, and for the longest time I secretly aspired to it as a career. I loved the idea of it, the freedom. I'd ask Papaw questions about it, and he'd laugh and tell a few stories. But he never went very deep. He told the funny stuff, but I always had the sense that he was holding back, perhaps trying to protect

me in some way, to help keep alive in me my childish innocence about life, and living.

≈◦≈

"He never talked much about them," my father says. He
and I are sitting in lawn chairs, looking out over the river.
I've come to share some of the pictures with him, to ask
him some of the questions that have taken so very long to
ask. It's been long enough, finally. Long enough for us to
at least try.

I'm asking him about Papaw, about what he was
like as a father, and what his parents were like. I'm trying to put together images in my head—of Papaw as a
young man, and Dad as his son. Trying to fill in the
blanks. Across the water we can see the TVA plant, hear
it rumbling softly. A massive flock of blackbirds flies
over us in a wave, a twisting tornado darkening the sky,
then passing and drifting toward the horizon like a vast
swirl of smoke.

"As long as I knew him, he never said one thing
about his own daddy," my father says, and he seems per-
plexed, as if just now realizing he had forgotten to ask the
right questions, back when there was still time to ask
them. It's difficult for both of us, talking about these
things, especially about Momma, though we pretend it is
not. He's all gray now, still handsome, quiet, less enam-
ored with life, perhaps, but not as gloomy since marrying
Betty, a friend for more than forty years. He shifts his
lanky frame, lights another cigarette, and looks out over
the water...

❦

Jim — 2 years — 1928
One of those weird, old baby pictures. Dad is
wearing a baby dress, and his head looks enor-
mous in relation to his body. What is it about the
photographs back then? The young adults have
faces like very old people. The children look like
grown-ups with small bodies. This one looks like
a baby doll with an adult face super-imposed...

Talmadge and Ruth's only son, James William, was born
in Ohio in 1926 and dragged through a number of states.
(There would be a second child born to Ruth, a girl, still-
born, rarely talked about. Once or twice Mamaw tried to
tell me about her, never getting very far before the hurt
and tears caused her to change the subject and move on to
something else.)

Life was difficult enough, and then in 1936 Ruth con-
tracted tuberculosis. For a full year she was in a sanitar-
ium, then another two years at home in bed. While Papaw
was at work, my father would run home from school during his lunch break to fix her something to eat, then rush
back to his studies.

Many years later, Mamaw would tell me of those long
and difficult days, and how the love and devotion of her
family helped get her through. She never talked much
about it, really. But once, in one of our special, separate
times together, she told me. Leaning in and sharing with me
in what seemed great confidence, she spoke of how Jesus

had stayed near her through that dark season, and how through almost constant prayer she had grown very close to Him, like best friends, and had asked Him to heal her.

"What did Jesus say?" I half-whispered, eyes full open.

Mamaw blinked, and began to smile, wonderingly. She took my hands in hers and placed them on her lap, our knees touching, her face very close to mine. And I could see the tears coming into her eyes as she whispered back—

"He said *Yes*."

Jim—1944
Standing in front of some unknown building. He's wearing his uniform, tall, rail-thin and serious-looking. His legs were so skinny his pants looked like narrow flags blowing in the breeze. His buddies called him "High Pockets"...

According to family legend, my mother was the first single female my father ever laid eyes on. Mamaw and Papaw were friends with another couple in Murray, Penny and Lyda Pentecost. When my father was born Lyda came for a visit to see the new baby, and brought along her one-year-old daughter. It was, however, something less than love at first sight; as Lyda lifted Mary Jo up above the crib for a look, this skinny little girl who was to become my mother seemed mostly unimpressed, and the infant destined to be my dad screamed bloody murder. Though later they would become friends in high school,

Mom and Dad never dated. Mary Jo was deeply in love with another boy named Willard Jarvis. There are still pictures of him in the box, square-jawed and serious, wearing an Air Force uniform.

Then the war. Apparently somewhat scarred by the childhood bouts of poverty, my father would complete four years' worth of college in two and a half, entering the Air Force Cadet Program as one of the youngest boys in state history ever to qualify. Dad never saw actual combat, but Willard Jarvis became a pilot and was killed in action. Upon returning home, Dad found Mary Jo stricken with grief. The two renewed their friendship, a relationship that later turned romantic.

"Did you fall in love?"—a silly question, and I feel stupid asking it.

"It just sort of happened."—putting out his cigarette—"It's hard to remember."

Easter, 1958 — Joette, 9 Years — Jimmy, 3 Years — Jennifer, 4 Months — West View Ave.
On the couch in the living room. Joette, blond hair curled and past her shoulders, long legs with white socks and white Sunday shoes, holding baby Jennifer in her lap. I'm wearing some cool striped suit with short pants and saddle oxfords...

None of us looked like we were their real children. It was a running gag—we must have been adopted or found on the doorstep, not seeming to resemble either parent. But they were so different, Mom and Dad, inside and out, that it was only natural we should turn out as physical and emotional hybrids—Dad, more than six feet tall, lanky and dark-haired, easy-going, thoughtful, gentle; Mom, a good foot shorter, petite, volatile, fair but full of fire. Night and day, the two of them, and perhaps why I've always felt torn, as if there were two different personalities inside me—why I've always relished playing other roles, other characters, never quite sure of my own. Maybe it's why my sisters are still to this day terrified of thunderstorms, and why I still can't help being fascinated by them, drawn dangerously close to them, staring into their darkness, wondering where they come from and where they're going. Maybe these polar differences, ever present, explain why I usually try to avoid conflict and use humor as a buffer when things really bother me, playing the family clown, stuffing my anger, always appearing calm on the surface while inwardly it's all unbridled emotion, laughing too loudly, crying too easily, screaming my silent screams…popular and attractive on the outside, yet always with the troubling, secret sense of something being broken on the inside. Sometimes the life of the party, other times isolating, depressed and full of fear. Maybe it's why when I take those personality profile tests I always come up both introvert and extrovert—not quite one and almost the other, longing for solitude, aching for companionship, terrified of commitment and betrayal, passive and passionate, spiritual and carnal, calmly crossing my arms like a wall while destroying the furniture within. Maybe it's why I feel so torn between the pious and the profane, never sure moment to moment if I'm running to God or from Him. And now, supposedly all grown up, still so often full of what feels like my mother's fury and fear, always holding it in, keeping it in check, with something of my father standing guard over it, over me. Born with my heart on my sleeve, buttoned tight at the cuff, caught somewhere between and engaged in persistent debate with my father, who could never quite bring himself to hit me, and with my mother, who could never quite keep herself from it.

Mary Jo and Lyda
No date. The writing looks like Mamaw's. It's a picture of Mom and Big Mama, standing near a white-framed house. Mom looks no more than twenty. They are smiling—Mom's flashing, like a movie star, Big Mama's reserved, almost cautious, lips tight and upturned against their will...

There are remarkably few pictures of my mother's parents. I've gone through the box again, and there just aren't many there. I know Big Mama was in the hospital a lot back then. Still, why so few? Maybe Mom ended up with some of them, and now they're lost. Or maybe her mom just didn't like to have her picture taken, afraid the camera might steal her soul.

Mary Jo Pentecost grew up, like my dad, an only child. I never really knew her father. He was successful, apparently a workaholic, and I have no real memories of him. They named me after him; his name was Eugene, but all of his friends called him Penny. Our family called him Big Daddy. He died of a massive heart attack at 62, walking home from work at lunchtime, right there on the sidewalk in front of their house. I was very young, but I remember being in my room on a cool, cloudy afternoon, and the sound of gravel being crushed under the tires of a car pulling into our driveway. A door opening, closing. Quiet. Then the sound of my mother's wails, primal and terrifying, sounds I had never heard before. It was as though our entire house was suddenly covered in a blue haze, and I knew the way children often know such things that something awful and life-changing had happened, and that we might never be the same. A part of me desperately wanted to run to her, to comfort her and make her smile again, make the house smile again, but an even stronger part of me was too afraid, and so I stayed in my room, hiding.

Please, God, make it stop.

Strange, the things we remember. Only once, briefly, did I ever really connect with her, the woman who gave birth to my mother. Big Mama and I never grew close. Despite a nickname I always thought better suited to some enormous biker queen, she was in fact a small, refined woman, bright and elegant-looking, but with a frightened place in her, something that made her always nervous and uneasy and difficult to be near. I loved her, of course, but always from a bit of a distance, always with a sense that something was not quite in balance—that she might tip over at any moment and break into pieces.

Big Mama carried with her, from childhood I assume, some eccentric beliefs. She in turn passed them on to her daughter, who then began teaching these "truths" to my sisters and me. Whenever Big Mama opened a new jar of sliced sweet pickles, for instance, she scraped away the top layer with a butter knife and threw it in the trash. It didn't matter if the pickles were store-bought or home made; this top layer was at high risk of having "turned." Once turned, they apparently became highly toxic, and eating even one could have disastrous results. She also taught my mother—who then taught us—that when taking a shower, shampooing hair should always be the final phase of the procedure. Otherwise, shampooing first, then letting our hair sit wet on our heads while washing the rest of our bodies, would put us at high risk for "Sour Scalp." We were never given a clear picture of what kind of poison the tainted top pickles produced, or what sort of horror awaited a victim of Sour Scalp. And even back then I secretly suspected that the overall logic of it all might be less than sound. Still, she was old—older than our own mother—and it seemed reasonable to think that she might therefore possess some ornate wisdom beyond my own.

Once taught fear, every headache becomes a potential brain tumor, every growing-pain a growing cancer.

The truth is, these "truths" we learn from our first "gods" can be difficult to dismiss; only in recent years have I been able to overcome my top-layer pickle aversion. And to this day I shampoo my hair last. Better safe than sorry.

I never really knew my grandmother at all; she was mostly unavailable, even when sitting in the same room with me, hands entangled in her lap like two spiders in a death-clench. But I have had with me always one vivid, never-fading connection to her, apparently meaningless on the surface, yet one that has for some reason survives the years when so much else has become mist. It is one of those inexplicable God-moments, perhaps meant as a gift, or a lesson. Or even a warning.

It was late fall, I think, because I remember the air feeling that way, and the sun lurking low in the sky, drawing heavy golden shadows across the ground. I was playing in the woods near our house, and I found a turtle—a real beauty, bigger than both my hands, with yellow diamond shapes on its shell. I rushed home carefully cradling the creature like a priceless treasure. Dashing through the door of our house, the first person I saw was Big Mama, standing in the kitchen, holding a glass of water.

"It's a TURTLE!"—Breathlessly, holding it up for her to see, unsure if she would fully appreciate my find. I rarely shared such things with her, but she seemed to be the only person there, and I had to show *someone*. And then the strangest thing happened. Big Mama looked at me, kindly but somewhat startled, and after a long, very still moment said:

"Well…what about its mother?"

I must have stopped panting, stopped breathing, and time seemed to pause, and the child-like excitement inside me turned into something else, something ominous, and all the joy ran out of me as if I'd been broken like glass. My face must have changed, because Big Mama seemed suddenly taken aback, her free hand fluttering toward her face like a moth, the thin, painted lips even more drawn.

"I mean," she started again, haltingly, "I mean… what will its mother do when she comes home and finds her…her baby missing?"

She was looking at me with her round, frightened eyes, perfect except for the dark shadows encircling them. And our eyes locked, hard and fast, and something like heavy, thick despair fell over us, right there in the kitchen with a water glass in her hand and a kidnapped turtle in mine. We were sharing something, I think, an unspoken and unspeakable longing, connected by some invisible sorrow that in a way belonged to us both, by blood perhaps. A familiar voice, a voice always whispering—*life is risky, joy is dangerous*—carrying with it an underlying sense of impending tragedy always and forever in everything…there, in her eyes…my eyes.

Her question penetrated me; I was struck dumb by some horrible truth in it. It was as if she had by accident broken in on my most private of places, the one I thought well-hidden within me, and had seen through my practiced pretending, recognizing me for who and what I really was. I felt as if I might suffocate, suddenly aware of big, embarrassing tears filling my eyes, and then hers. It had little to do with turtles, probably, this strange whatever-it-was passing between us in that remarkable instant, and everything to do with her own haunted heart and mine—touching, meshing somehow, somewhere—for the briefest and most blinding of moments, our souls fully revealed.

Looking up. Seeing each other, through our tears, clearly, for the first and only time. Then, as if she felt sorry for what she had said, she reached out her hand to me, but I was gone, out the door, now driven by a mission of mercy. I flew through the woods, the clean wind driving more tears across my cheeks, wondering if I could find the place where I had made my discovery—*Oh God. Please let me find it, and please let the mother find her baby. If she's been looking, please don't let her give up. I'm bringing him…I'm bringing him home…*

Until, finally, into a cool shade, feeling the familiar moss like springs under my feet. Satisfied I'd found the same tree, I gently placed the lost child on the ground at its base, home at last. There were no other turtles in sight, and this one, still hiding inside its shell, looked tiny and helpless, sitting there beneath this huge pine, the sun nearly gone. I backed away, slowly, unsure, then turned and ran, desperately back to my own home, not daring to look back.

Big Mama and I never spoke of it again, to each other or to anyone else. And I don't recall any other occasions when either of us made the effort to draw closer. Perhaps it was the death of her husband, or maybe she had always been that way, but there was in Big Mama a hurt that never seemed to heal, a place my sisters and I were reluctant to approach. She possessed a quality of quiet desperation that shadowed her always, as though she were pursued by a sort of self-fulfilling prophecy of a life destined for tragedy.

We children were never told about it while she was alive. But later we would learn about the "mental hospitals," mostly by overhearing hushed voices from the next room, half-whispers of this family "curse" my mother so feared. Big Mama died when I was a teenager, but that same ghost of fear that had lived inside her never left our family, returning in the face of someone I knew better than anyone, turning her into someone I could barely recognize.

Jim — Setting Up Office — (No Date)
Still skinny as a beanpole. Someone rented him the basement of their office building, a perfect place for the town's first "eye doctor" to set up shop. He's leaning over his shiny new examination chair, the one he'd sometimes let me pretend was a spaceship, pressing his foot on the magic button...up, down, up, down...

I loved it when Mom would take us for a visit at The Office. It was always very cool inside, and smelled of something not quite like medicine, a pleasant yet very serious smell, strange and professional. Dad would give me rides in the chair, and let me look through the machine that projected colored letters onto a screen attached to the wall. He looked very important in his white lab coat, flipping the lenses around on the machine, moving through a mock eye examination for me. I always felt as though I had to be very quiet in the office, as if it were a sacred place. I thought being an optometrist must be a very important thing.

Our father was determined, I suppose, never to feel hungry again, or have his children do without the comforts of life. He worked a lot. He built a solid practice, made good money, and took care of his family, including his own parents; he bought Mamaw and Papaw a little house within walking distance of our own. For a while, after his work had reached full steam, Dad would buy a new Thunderbird every year, trading in the "old" one. He was always buying things, trying to make Mom—all of us—smile. And we'd come squealing out of the house when he pulled into the driveway, and sit inside as if it were a magic carriage, working the space-age electric windows up and down, filling our lungs with the smell of leather and plastic and glue and rubber. For a while, it really was magic. But the new-car smell never lasted long.

Deer Country—October 1962

Don't know what "Deer Country" means. Daddy liked to hunt back then, and maybe he suggested what to write on the back of the picture. Beautiful land. Someone (Mamaw or Papaw?) snapped it of the five of us. We're out in the country somewhere, on a gravel road. Leaning against the front bumper of a white car; can't make out the model, maybe a Pontiac? Behind us lies a huge open field, and beyond that, thick woods. Mom's hair is short and curly; Joette is standing between Mom and

Dad, looking awkward and self-conscious, wearing those awful-looking cat-eye glasses, her teeth in braces. Jennifer is in front of Mom, posing the way she always did, arms at her side, tentative smile, the glass-hearted kid. I'm in front of Dad, and he has his hands on my shoulders. We're showing off our matching flat-tops...

He was cool, my dad. He could belch like thunder. He could take a blade of grass, and holding it in some secret way between his thumbs and blowing into cupped hands, create his screeching "peacock mating call" whistle that could be heard for blocks.

I liked to watch him drive a car—solid, safe and sure, rarely going over the speed limit, always setting a good example. He showed me how to correctly hold the steering wheel, hands at 10 and 2, "just like a clock." He was funny, but smart. Watching him interact with his friends always gave me a warm feeling of pride, because I saw him as a balanced blend of things: intelligent but humble, as interested in things scientific and artistic as in duck hunting and sports, comfortable with all sorts of different personalities. I can feel and see him in myself now—the way I use humor to disarm people, my tendency to be goofy one moment and serious the next, my external ease with people from all walks of life. He taught me that there is nothing mutually exclusive about appreciating fancy big city dining one meal and good barbecue the next.

I was never more proud than when he and I would sit together on a Sunday afternoon, watching football on TV, eating sardines and Vienna sausages and saltine crackers. It took me a while to get used to the sardines, but Dad loved them, and so I vowed to love them, too. It was a very special time, downstairs in the den, just the two of us, eating guy food and talking guy talk. Whenever my beloved Dallas Cowboys were playing, we whooped and hollered as Dandy Don Meredith hit Bullet Bob Hayes with a bomb.

"They'll never catch him!" my dad would yell, and I'd be on my feet, wide-eyed and screaming as "the world's fastest human" streaked the length of the field, leaving lesser men flailing helplessly in his wake. Those were good days, there together, the burnished gold shadows of fall coming through the windows, me and my dad, Big Jim and Little Jim, laughing and eating sardines.

I remember so many things about my father. But, oddly, I don't recall his ever being angry. He could get frustrated, of course. And his booming voice would throttle us into immediate obedience. But I never saw him truly angry, or out of control. I don't know if anger was an emotion that had been forbidden him since childhood, or if over time it had become something he forbade himself. Maybe it was a part of him he just never let us see.

One day he took me to get a flat-top hair cut, just like his, at Tater's Barber Shop on the Court Square. We sat side by side in the only two barber chairs in town, the sun streaming in, the smell of soap and blue antiseptic and cigar smoke making me feel grown-up and important.

"How 'bout the full treatment, Tater?" Dad said. "For both of us." And my chest swelled as I had my first "shave"—big, bald Tater wrapping steaming hot towels over my face, then the warm creamy lather, masterfully whisking it away with the dull side of a straight razor.

Then, red-faced and resolute, I marveled as the buzzing thing in his hand transformed me into a small version of my father. Soon the two of us had short hair sticking straight up, gooey with Butch Wax.

When we were done, Dad picked me up and held our faces close together in front of the mirror. I felt proud beyond words.

When I grew a bit older, Dad took me duck hunting. Momma was very concerned that I would freeze to death, and she had every right. The Camden Bottoms are a beautiful but primitive place, and there has never been a spot on this planet or any other as numbingly cold in the dead of winter; even with my back turned to the wind, moving across the river in a small metal boat before dawn, I could feel the breath-stealing sting, though my mother had bundled me in so many layers of clothing I could barely move my arms and legs. I must have had six pairs of socks on my feet, and still after only fifteen minutes in that duck blind I had no feeling in my toes. I learned that day that hunting was never going to be a passion. Shooting the gun was cool, but freezing was no fun at all. Still, I didn't want him to know that I wasn't enjoying myself, so I tried not to complain, to tough it out, to be one of the boys.

He took me dove hunting once, too, and I crouched beside him in a corn field, shaking as the shots rang out from invisible hunters all around us, the lead pellets falling down on our hats like gentle rain. I was afraid, but

I didn't want him to know. I enjoyed nature, but didn't like killing things. I loved football, but I loved literature, too, and was as easily impressed by a famous painter as I was by Bullet Bob. I liked sardines, but something in me longed for the flavor of things not yet tasted, exotic things, experiences that lay beyond the limits of my little town. Like my father, I was just a bit different.

I'm not at all sure what some of my father's grown-up hopes and desires were back then. But I suppose in many ways his dreams were once upon a time very similar to my own. Like me, he had once been just a boy, running, running fast, imagining many things, and dreaming many dreams. And, for both of us, many of them never came true.

Boy Scout, Troop 22—Junior High Marching Band, Trumpet—High School Football, #42

Pulling out more photographs, sifting through handfuls of them. There was so much good in my life back then, so many more sunny days than stormy ones. Faith came easily, effortlessly. My life was a privileged one. Countless memories make me smile. And yet, the good of my past couldn't completely insulate me, or keep me from going through life with my hand always poised above a button marked "Self-Destruct."

The pictures. I can't help thinking that in many of them I appear to be trying very, very hard—young, smiling, hopeful. Always joining, wearing the uniforms, trying to fit in, to be a part of something that worked. To prove myself, maybe, to test my mettle. Forever trying to achieve the unattainable, hoping the next thing would do it, would in some way complete me, perhaps. Trying to find a place that fit, a place where I might finally belong. Hoping to audition for and win the role of a lifetime, in some sort of a family.

A well and whole family.

the big game

Jimmy—New Uniform
The day before my first real game. New glove big
as my head, hanging on the end of my skinny arm.
I'd been hitting the ball pretty good up to then.
Ready to play, to show what I could do...

I was little. But I could *run*. Fast as a jackrabbit, flat feet
and all. I discovered in school that I could outrun my

longer-legged classmates. This came as a big surprise to everyone, since there was some concern early on that something might be wrong with me; I took what seemed a good long time learning to walk, and even then I didn't seem to have it down quite right. Worried by the weird wobble of my walk as a toddler, my parents had finally taken me to a "bone specialist" in Nashville. From the sound of his title, I had visions of someone down deep in a dungeon laboratory, performing morbid experiments on humans, skeletons hanging from the ceiling. I pictured a skinny, scary guy, like Doctor Frankenstein.

As it turned out, he was a normal-looking person. My feet were x-rayed from every angle. "In twenty years of medicine," the Doctor spoke solemnly, his glasses perched professionally on the end of his nose, "these are the flattest feet I've ever seen." They put rounded pieces of metal covered with adhesive cloth inside some heavy, stiff black "corrective" shoes, and sent us away with instructions that I should wear them every day. I dutifully laced them up every morning before leaving our house, then pulled them off once I hit the woods, running barefoot.

And then one day at recess all the boys had a big race, from the monkey bars to the swings, and I won. The bigger boys claimed I'd left early, or that they'd slipped, so we did it again. And I won again. Suddenly, I had become the new champ—running and winning, fastest kid on the playground, unaware of my handicap, soaring clueless as a bumblebee. Something in me rejoiced in this revelation, knowing that running, *running fast,* was something I could do *well*. And out there, leading the pack with the wind in my face, my feet barely touching the ground, I knew this was as close to flying as I would ever get, on the waking side of my dreams.

My dad was a good baseball player. Once, on a fine summer day, with all the dads playing a benefit game at the park to raise money for the Little League teams, *my* dad hit a home run. All the other kids slapped me on the back, and I just sat there, speechless and amazed. Then, as he touched home plate and headed for the dugout, he smiled and pointed straight at me in the stands.

"Jimbo!" he yelled. "You wanna see me hit one left handed?" And next time up, he did it—a line shot right over the Rexall Pharmacy sign in left centerfield. My father ran, easy and smooth. As he rounded third base, nearing home, he raised his arms in the air, like an eagle preparing to land, like Captain America leaping from the top of a building. The little crowd cheered. And then my father's eyes found me again, and he smiled, and gave me a thumbs-up. I could feel my heart pounding.

I don't think I ever told him so, but on that day he made me feel like *I* was flying.

I wanted to play baseball, just like my dad. It became my dream to round the bases one fine day, arms raised, the crowd roaring—a hero, like him. The night before my first practice game as a Little Leaguer, I felt ready and confident. Dad had been helping me, teaching me to throw and catch and hit. Mom had taken me to the Dime Store and bought me some shredded bubble gum in a pouch, just like chewing tobacco. And I had my new uniform, gray with shiny green stripes. It lay folded in a chair, right beside my bed. I'd already buttoned up my chew in the back pocket of my pants.

That night the rain woke me, pounding on the roof. I lay there and prayed for it to stop, then fell asleep. But the next morning I felt Mom leaning over me, rubbing my head. "Game's rained out, honey," she said. "Coach just called." She tried to cheer me up, encouraging me to put on the uniform anyway and play outside in my yard. But it wasn't the same. Dad was at work, and the ground was too wet, and I just ended up getting my new uniform all dirty. Later, Mom accidentally put it in the washing machine with the chew still in the pocket, and that only made things worse.

I languished all that season with the other beginners on the B-Teams, mostly chasing butterflies around the outfield. But apparently, because I could run so fast and cover so much ground trying to catch insects, the next year the coaches decided to move me up to A-Team with the older kids a year early. Papaw said it was a sign of future greatness. It would prove my undoing.

I sat on the bench, at first. Every game. Then one night, for reasons I cannot explain, the coach decided to pinch-hit me. And this was not just *any* game. *Joe Baxter was pitching.*

I'd been watching him all night from the dugout. He was a Benton County legend. Tall, absurdly tall, legs too long for his uniform, arms that hung to his knees, a big, lanky, soft-spoken country boy with a fastball about which many a tall story had been told. And there he stood, *the* Joe Baxter, several years older than me, towering on the mound like some mythical giant.

When I heard the coach call out my name, I thought he was kidding. But he just sat there, looking right at me, waiting. I grabbed a bat and walked to the plate, as if in a dream. A sort of amused murmur started in the crowd, building into a collective chuckle.

I must have looked like a midget. My uniform covered me like a tent. My over-sized batting helmet wobbled around on my head as I walked to the plate, and I felt like one of those bobble-head dolls I'd seen through the back windshields of cars in town. I stepped into the batter's box, fascinated and fearful—the lights giving a surreal look to the field, summer hanging heavy in the night air, moths the size of small sparrows bouncing off the mercury-vapor bulbs, the opposing players chattering, making fun—*no batta no batta, check out short-stuff, whose the shrimp? NO BATTA!*—the bigger guys slowly realizing the humor in this one, the chatter turning to amused catcalls and worse. Everyone was having fun with it, even the crowd. I wondered what my family was thinking. They were all there—and Papaw, too, who never missed a game, standing in his regular spot behind home plate, bony brown fingers laced through the chicken wire backstop. I knew they were watching.

Looking up. From the mound, he seemed hundreds of feet above me. I can still see the look on Joe Baxter's face as he stared in to the catcher for the sign, deadly-serious, concentrated. Then, getting a good look at me, a

moment of disbelief, followed by a sort of half-grin and—
what, *compassion?* He took off his cap and wiped his forehead, then put it back on, a very used cap, a real player's
cap, faded and perfectly formed to his head, a relaxed, pro-
fessional-looking piece of equipment. And watching him do
that—take off the cap, wipe his face, put it back on, all one
smooth, effortless motion, a thing of great style and beauty,
an artist and his instrument moving as one piece, one
flesh—watching him do that one simple thing made me feel
absurd, and utterly inconsequential…

Remembering. Why this one night, this one moment?
The near-perfect detail, as if it had happened yesterday
instead of forty years ago…so vivid, even now the taste of
it still in my mouth, the damp night heavy in my lungs,
everything slowed so that I can see it, feel the red clay
between my cleats and the sag in my uniform…

He was back to business, rubbing up the ball, staring
past me into the catcher, ignoring me. Straightening, into
the windup. There was absolutely no chance—none—of
my hitting the ball he was about to throw. I knew that. I
would not be able to even swing the bat, much less hit a
home run the way I had envisioned so many times in my
dreams. I was destined to look ridiculous, in front of the
whole town, and there wasn't a thing I could do about it.
It was too late now. I stood there, frozen as much by
shame as by fright, wanting to run away, watching Joe
Baxter in slow motion lifting one leg and curling his lanky
frame into an impossible shape, then, poised for a moment
at the peak of his windup, motionless, one eye trained on
me like a hawk on its prey…and then, watching wide-eyed

from underneath the dubious protection of my helmet, I saw the briefest glimpse of the white ball from somewhere within the tangled, giant spider-mass of arms and legs... the right arm swinging wide and free, at least six feet long, swinging toward me, the ball leaving his fingers seemingly inches from my face.

That was the last thing I saw. I heard a loud pop, and heard the Ump yell STEEE-RIKE ONE! I looked at the catcher. He was holding the ball, grinning at me, then casually tossing it back. Now the chatter really got bad, and the locals were having the time of their lives. Joe Baxter rubbed up the ball, and as he turned back to the mound I saw him glance at the third baseman; both of them were smiling and shaking their heads. I felt like an ant.

Remembering. Out of all the dozens of games and hundreds of nights...this one night—"Come on, Jimmy! Get a hit!"—It was Mom. I could hear her yelling from the crowd. I was wondering where Dad was sitting...

And then I really do remember. *This night*—when I *knew*, when I felt something like heavy shadow fall on me, when I experienced the suffocating truth of separateness, of profound detachment, at once both the center of attention and yet entirely removed, as if viewing it all from some indefinable, dislocated distance. Suddenly, I had the sure feeling that Dad, Mom, Papaw, and even God were separated from me by far more than chicken wire. Standing there surrounded by the chatter and the smell of dirt and chalk, the dew glimmering like diamonds on the fresh-mown grass and the ethereal banging of giant moths against the lights, I became aware of some vast, impassable chasm between my private world and the one into which I had mistakenly been born. I felt both superior and lost, above it all but less than enough—not simply young and afraid, but certain beyond all doubt that *I did not belong*. And stranded there at home plate with half the town watching, the bat resting uselessly on my shoulder, I felt fully what to some extent I have always felt—very small, and very *lonely*.

...*He was winding up again.* And the white streak was coming at me, right at me, and I could do nothing but shut my eyes tight. This time it was more a thud than a pop. The ball hit me square on the left forearm.

It must have been some pitch other than the mythical fastball from Joe Baxter's arsenal that struck me; otherwise, I'm sure my arm would have been broken. There was a sudden hush from the crowd, the whole field silent. I stood there, staring at my arm, waiting for the pain, though it now seemed to be someone else's arm. Joe Baxter came a few steps off the mound, his long, friendly face suddenly concerned—a strange moment, with me still at center stage, but no one was laughing anymore. And then there were people pressing in all around me, amazed that I could still be alive after encountering this most deadly of things. And for days afterward people would want to look at the bruise on my arm, saying stuff like—*Wow! Is this where Joe Baxter's pitch hit you? Wow.*

I never got over it. For the rest of my childhood I couldn't hit a baseball. We tried extra coaching and eventually even a fancy mechanical pitching machine, but nothing worked. Still fast, I played for several more years, but rarely did more than pinch-run or play late innings in the outfield. For the most part, I didn't care much for baseball after that. I still don't.

I never blamed Joe Baxter. I blamed that rainstorm, the one that kept me from being in that practice game, the game scheduled in the bright of day, with no crowd leering down. I blamed the rain that turned my Big League Chew into a sticky wad and ruined my shiny new pants. And God was in charge of the rain.

The taste of fear. Fear of the baseball, afraid of being hurt, of being small, of being laughed at. Even more, that night seemed to validate what I had been suspecting for so long. I became more convinced than ever that being afraid—the kind of afraid I'd been feeling for as long as I could remember—was going to be the natural way of things for me, for the rest of my life. A generic and perhaps genetic fear of being inexplicably disconnected, and with it the subtle but persistent panic of being lost. Of somehow being *at* the Big Game, but not *in* it.

Of course, it had very little to do with that one night, that one game; I had learned the fear already, in my own home. Still, it seemed as though a face that had been forever lurking inside my heart had come closer to the surface, creeping like some dark thing into my secret room and shaking me from a soft and secure sleep, trying to stir me from a deep dream.

Vacation—Smokies, 1963
The five of us, standing on top of the mountain. Behind us you can see the chair lift, and beyond that the mists hanging over the rich green valley far below. Dad must have asked some stranger to take our picture. We look happy. We're all smiling. Everyone looks okay, even Mom. I can't help noticing what a good-looking family we were then, just the way a family should look...the way I liked to think of us then, the way I like to think of us now...

The way I think of us. On and on, more baby pictures, family vacations in the mountains and on the beach, my little sister and I dressed up for Halloween, school plays, picnics, Christmas mornings and birthday parties and high school annuals. I sit like some poor fool caught red-handed in a Kodak Moment, nostalgically strolling through time.

Stuck somewhere between remembering and forgetting. I have no recollection of having my tonsils removed when I was seven. But the wretched smell of ether pressed onto my face will sometimes even now come drifting back to me, a faint but horrible thing, turning my stomach. Only small snatches of images from our family vacations remain, and yet I can see vividly the afternoon I fell and hit my head on a rock. They kept watch over me through the night, making sure I didn't have a concussion, our planned trip to the beach the following morning now in doubt. What if we couldn't go? I wouldn't see the ocean;

none of us would. I wailed and moaned. It would be my fault. All my fault.

I remember the love and joy in our house. I can still see my mother's smile, and feel the warmth rising inside my chest at the sound of her laughter. And I can remember how much fun she could be. That's all I've ever wanted to remember. For the longest time I've quickly looked the other way when, unexpectedly turning a corner in my mind, I come upon her lying there on the couch, not moving, one arm hanging loosely down, fingers curled and lightly touching the floor...her eyes half-closed, mouth open...walking silently toward her, holding my breath, reaching out my hand across the cold chasm between us, toward her pale face...

I thought she was dead.

If we ever dare hope to capture and tell time—to even hold it still long enough to get a good look at it, much less describe what it was and what it did for us and to us— and if all we have are these moments crammed into a box full of curling photographs, then perhaps the only thing we can do is grab onto them and stare deeply into them, if not to make sense of what we see, then at least to pray it might all somehow make sense of us. But the rest of it, the *real* of it, I'll have to remember on my own. There are very few photographs that tell of the place and time where my journey must take me now—where the years were spent in dim shadows, without enough light to expose the images. I'll have to go back and live there, again, and stop playing the Big Game. All these years, helplessly holding in my heart my own precious portrait, unchanging, the one showing the sparkle in her eyes. The rest had nearly vanished.

The family pictures have said all they have to say, really, at least for now. I pick out a few more to look at later, ones that make me smile, and the rest I put back in the box.

The rain has stopped. I take my cup of coffee and walk into the backyard. *Looking up.* Fall is coming, the leaves near the tops of the maples just shading to yellow. That faint chill is sneaking into the air, the smell of change, of time passing. And without realizing that I'm even feeling sad, tears start coming. I have to sit down, right there in the wet grass. It's not nostalgia, or even regret, really. It's knowing, somehow, that it's finally time to go back. All the way back.

The things we remember. Lying under that oak tree, calling out His name as if He were the only real friend I had in the world. Maybe our memories are markers, like bread crumbs discreetly dropped along the path, clues glimmering in the moonlight by which we hope one night to find our way back home, back to Him...these handful of images that have followed us closely all through our lives, unchanging, never aging, not in the least dimmed by time. Like the rope swing. Or a simple lullaby...*Matthew, Mark, Luke and John...*

Or the times, when lying alone in my bed at night listening to the rain at the window or, when there was no rain, to the sound of my own beating heart, I would hear the low, murmured sounds of my parents' voices in the next room. And in a clear, simple way, I knew something was wrong. There was often a different sound to their words. I couldn't make out what they were saying, but I knew they were speaking of things I wasn't supposed to hear, sharing truths between them that they would not or could not share with me. Like the wind of a distant storm their voices would rise and fall, rise and fall, and silently I shared with Him about how frightened I was, about how I wanted them to stop fighting. And I would ask Him for the courage to get out of bed and go into the other room and make them hold me, make them love me, and so somehow make them love each other for ever and ever, but I couldn't do it, and would lie there frozen beneath my warm quilts, eyes shut tight...

Please, God, make them stop.

And He would always comfort me in His voiceless, strong-soft sort of way, until I soon fell asleep in His arms. And I dreamed with Him, and in so dreaming became tall and brave.

*I dreamed I was running, running fast...*racing through this place called childhood, dancing barefoot, barely touching the ground. The few images that remain seem now less than a moment, a caught breath, a missed heart-beat, almost nothing and nearly everything, invulnerable as they are brief. One day dreaming with our toes in the mud and a blade of grass in our teeth, then suddenly, mer-cilessly wide awake, our innocence lost, with no apparent way back. Like all children who wake one morning to find the summer gone, I sit under a gray sky in green grass turning brown, aching for something lost. And within me there is a heartbreaking gratitude for the things we remember, and a deep mourning for the things we forget.

We grow up. Some of us do, anyway, without meaning to or knowing how it happens. We sometimes take the light God has given and turn it into something else, something dark and caved in upon itself, something heartless and selfish and cruel. We leave our little towns, however large or small, and our families, however bright or broken, and go to distant countries, wandering after other gods.

For a long time, I did not seem to miss Him much. I put my thoughts of Him away somewhere and just went on ahead alone. I don't know why or even exactly when, but one day I simply turned away and didn't look back. Then, many grown-up years later, after traveling a road no one could have predicted, I would find myself once again calling out His name, crying to Him from the ground, looking up, scraped and bleeding and frightened, the rope swinging loose and out of reach above me from a branch too high to imagine. And I would learn, just in time, that there are both God-Dreams and dreams of our own making, and that those who have tasted His need never be lost to the other.

≈ *Part Two* ≈
waking

Vain hopes
are often like
the dreams
of those who wake.
—*Quintilian*

"Stop your nonsense, Wilbur!"
said the oldest sheep.
"...the quickest way
to spoil a friendship
is to wake somebody up
in the morning
before he is ready."
—*E. B. White*
Charlotte's Web

the children

Watson Street, Spring 1960
The two of us, sitting side by side on the white
bench swing, in the shade of a maple tree. Behind
us, her rose bushes wind and twine themselves
around a white wood trellis. Mamaw has her arm
around me...

We'd walk up "the back way," my little sister and I, a
brave and exciting journey for such short legs, though

really consisting of only about four back yards. *Smells*: brownies, jams, cookies, homemade candy. In spring and summer, the perfume of fresh pink blossoms from her rose bushes, and Jergen's Lotion (the original scent in the white bottle), and drifting from somewhere on the side porch mingled the musty-smoky smells of Papaw's tobacco and coffee.

We shared the simplest things together, singing, taking walks, or sitting on the little screened porch watching the dusk creep over the trees and grass, listening to the crickets echoing their song off the deepening sky...not speaking, hypnotized, the lucent lightning bugs floating and shimmering like fairies through the soft southern summer night.

We shared long and humid days in the backyard garden, clearing and planting, Papaw teaching me how deep to dig and how to drop in the seed. My least favorite job was pulling weeds. Mamaw would ask me to help, and I'd set my feet and begin grunting and pulling, some of the weeds taller than me. She'd watch a while and laugh, finally coming to my rescue.

"Looks like you could use some help," she'd say.

She has one foot on the ground, keeping the swing moving, just enough, an effortless and subtle movement of her toes, smooth and slow, the creaking of the chains steady as a heartbeat...

This one doesn't feel like a memory at all. It feels like part of the texture of me now, as if it might have happened only a few hours ago, this morning perhaps. The two of us, sitting on her white wooden swing in the backyard, talking about the birds. For hours, listening, occasionally discussing what kind of song we had heard, and which bird might have sung it.

"Who is that?" she would ask, and I'd listen again, closely, for the music coming from high in the branches.

"Cardinal? Bob White?"

"No, silly! Bob White sings his name." And laughing there together, the rusty chain of the swing creaking its own rhythmic song, we held time in our hands, knowing that for us, at least, it could never, *never* run out.

We're up very early one morning, just the two of us. Sitting on the porch, staring out into that not-dark, not-light time, the suspended moments before dawn. It is our special time, this sweet stillness, this pause, this holy space separating when the crickets stop their music and the birds begin their own, as if God were taking a deep breath.

"*Listen,*" she whispers.

And I hear the silence. The deafening anticipation. Nothingness. Waiting, as if for some command. We sit there, she and I, breathlessly listening for the heartbeat of creation. Just before the birds start singing.

One, two, several. Their song at first tentative, warming up, then a chorus sweeping out of the trees, perfectly unrehearsed, warm and reassuring. For several minutes, we do not speak.

"How do they know?" I ask, finally. And she smiles.

"God tells them," she says. "God tells them when to sing."

~≈>≈

Looking up.

In Mamaw's bedroom, lying on the spindle bed that had belonged to her mother, the bed that had traveled by covered wagon from North Carolina to Kentucky in a time long ago. Looking up at the pictures on the wall, framed reproductions of famous Christian paintings, which I remember still for a kind of fascinating attraction that went far beyond the inexpensive prints themselves and into something more, something I did not have to ask about, and something she never felt the need to explain.

The little one, my favorite, hung just above the light switch in a tiny wooden frame, small enough to fit in my hand. She had cut it out of a magazine, I think—a picture of a white dove in flight, its wings blurred in movement. The picture mesmerized me. Often, Mamaw took it from the wall and let me hold it. I would stare at it for the longest time; I thought it one of the most precious things I had ever seen.

And there was a picture of Jesus, too. He had long brown hair, soft and full, like the women in shampoo commercials. He held a baby lamb in the crook of his arm. He was beautiful and flawless, and not at all real-looking, and the picture had a sepia-tone softness about it, as if the paint had been brushed on with angel wings. It made me sleepy when I looked at it. Mamaw said that no matter from what part of the room you looked at the picture, His eyes would follow—"Like He's always watching you," she'd say. And I tried it, often, taking Him in from different angles. I could never tell for sure.

On a little table by the bed she always kept the latest copy of The Upper Room, a devotional booklet, and I would leaf through the miniature pages and absorb things from it long before I had any real idea of what it all meant. I can't remember Mamaw ever really *saying* much about salvation. Still, she was an evangelist in the truest sense. She reflected Him. I didn't know it then—and I would not fully understand it for a very long time—but in all the things we did together, in all the laughter and play and love we shared, she was preparing me. I was being saved.

Mamaw dreamed with me. She seemed from the beginning to sense my creative spirit, and she helped cultivate it. And this was the best part: *She knew about my Best Friend*. She seemed to understand, and being filled with the same light, she knew instinctively what to do. We sang and danced and read books and told stories. I began to recite poetry long before I could read or write it down, so she would transcribe my rhymes onto scraps of paper and keep them "forever" in a little wooden box.

> DOUBLEMINT, DENTENE
> SPEARMINT TOO
> TASTE SO GOOD
> AND GOOD TO CHEW

went one of my more memorable works, and I can see her beautiful gray eyes opening wide, her lips curled around a gasp of pure admiration.

"Beautiful!" she breathed. And from the very truest part of her, she meant it.

Always acting, always being someone else. I liked pretending. I became good at it. Superheroes like the Human Torch, sports stars like Bullet Bob Hayes, adventure guys from TV shows like Tarzan, Ilya Kuryakin on The Man From U.N.C.L.E., or James West on The Wild Wild West. I'd play Dad's old LPs or Joette's 45rpm records and lip-sync with the songs, pretending to be Elvis or The Beatles, a tennis racket as my guitar. I portrayed every character in Peter And The Wolf, the scratchy sounds blaring from a thick, brown 78rpm record—the innocent skip of Peter, the menacing stalk of the wolf, the brave and triumphant strut of the hunters—fascinated by how the different instruments infused their vivid imagery to each character: the bird-flute, the bassoon-duck, the orchestra swelling into its joyful heroic march after the wolf had met his fate. The music gave me chill-bumps. Lost in its world, lifting my knees high as I paraded through the imaginary city streets, I felt *victorious*.

I usually did these things only in private, of course, because I knew people would make fun of me. But Mamaw inspired me, and with her encouragement as fuel I created and performed plays for her, making up the stories as I went along, leaping melodramatically from chair to footstool to couch. If my performance was particularly pleasing to her, she might on very rare occasion treat me to her own magnum opus.

"Close your eyes and count to ten," she'd say. I knew what was coming, and still my pulse raced. Then, a cry—

"NOW!" And fearfully opening my eyes, I would gaze upon her wide, gummy smile...her teeth held before me in the palm of her hand! Invariably, I ran screaming through the house in mock horror, my grandmother clutching at her side in terrifying, toothless laughter.

With her, my imagination could soar. She gave wings to it. She let me be *alive*. And even years later, when my artistic leanings were beginning to cause concern for those who had been patiently waiting for me to "grow up," she remained encouraging. Never once did she make me feel foolish, even when I was clearly acting that way.

Mamaw *knew*.

"My bright-eyed Jimmy," she'd say, as if sharing a secret. "You're my special one." Whether or not her praise for me had to do with a real knowledge of some gift I possessed but did not yet understand, or simply functioned to build my character through encouragement, I can never be sure. But she always told me the truth, and so I absorbed what she said, and thought it true. She had lived a simple life. I don't know if she ever dreamed of stardom or of being famous, but within her shone the light that enables people to *be* those things. I thought she must *know something*, and of course she did. She knew.

She taught me to be still. Somehow, she could cause me to pause, and wait, there in the crook of her arm, for the reluctant end of the day, my energy winding down with the setting sun, the back porch slowly growing gray and smoke-blue and then dark...and a chorus of cicadas shimmering with night-song, surging, slowly rising to a roar, dense and deafening in the heavy, humid blackness...then backing away, then rising again, tirelessly rolling in on our little screened shore like the waves of some mighty, living sea.

I cannot search for clues to the origin of my childhood closeness with God without seeing her face. I'm not about to move through the landscape of my memories, hoping to catch a glimpse of my Best Friend, without holding her hand. As I journey back towards the Holy Source of my dreams, I find her at my side. She had a heart full of song. And she taught mine how to sing.

Mamaw and I invented a game. We called it "Getting Lost," and the rules were this: She and I would climb into the old Rambler Classic, a square white car that Papaw always said could only do forty or fifty miles an hour, tops, "downhill with a good wind behind it." Mamaw at the wheel, I would shout my commands: left, right, straight, or back. She *had* to go the direction I ordered; it was the rule of the game. During these half-day-long excursions it was my responsibility to lead us into the darkest, most remote, uninhabited, treacherous areas of rural Benton County. And we found plenty. In our minds, the more dangerous looking the little gravel road, the deeper into a thick wood where even the summer sun could barely reach and with the most disorienting assortment of twists and turns leading into a Land That Time Forgot, the more exciting the adventure became. In other words: the scarier, the better.

She'd be puttering along in that old Rambler, fearlessly manning the helm, when without warning I'd scream "TURN LEFT HERE!" or "STRAIGHT THROUGH THAT GATE!" or "BACK UP! LET'S GO BACK TO THAT MUD ROAD!" And, laughing in the face of danger, decades before the age of Fix-a-Flat or cell phones, we two explorers tried our best to get as lost as we possibly could.

Many years later, when she thought me old enough to know the truth, she confided that more than once during these expeditions she had been terrified we might never be able to return to civilization, doomed to spend the rest of our lives roaming the virtually uninhabited hills of middle Tennessee. At least until the gas ran out, or something horrible beyond description caught and ate us. I then admired her even more, of course, because I realized that though she had been afraid we might never find our way home, her fear never forced her to abandon the quest and turn back. She had promised to boldly go with me where no five-year-old had gone before, and go we did. Often I worried we were going to get lost, or break down, or be swept under in those low-lying woods by some evil flood or avalanche. But it never happened. Mamaw said Jesus was with us. And I felt safe with the two of them.

My grandmother possessed that marvelous combination of faith and wild abandon that all children have, and she knew instinctively the difference between living with daring and passion and living recklessly. She liked to have *fun*. She was gracefully childlike rather than childish, responsive to the music within her. And she cultivated in me the same stuff. *Never, never, never be afraid to dream*—her memory seems to be constantly saying—*Just tell me which way to turn. It's better to be lost and frightened than to never try a new road.*

And so we would go, deeper and deeper in to the unknown places, further down the path of pure, exhilarating faith, until the canopy of oak and pine and maple and sycamore thickened and the sky disappeared, day becoming night, a very young boy sliding ever closer along the Rambler's bench seat till he was snug against his favorite girl, both of them clinging to an invincible friendship. And as we went further into those dim and mysterious places, the gravel growling menacingly beneath the tires, the sun now no more than an occasional glimmer of hope, Mamaw and I would press our spirits and our courage and our dreams together, bound by a faith much stronger than our fear.

If right now I could go back to any time and to any place, I would go *there*. Pulling on an old pair of jeans and a T-shirt, I'd walk—no, *run,* like a wild deer—up the back way to her house, my feet wet in the dew-cold grass. Dashing through the back porch screen door, racing through the warm air of coffee and tobacco and into the sweet smell of bacon and eggs and buttered cinnamon toast, I would rush to her and smother myself in her apron, holding on for dear life, squeezing her and laughing and crying and thanking Heaven for another chance to show her how much I loved her. *"Jimmy? Jimmy? How can this be?"*—her eyes filling, but—*"There's no time now,"* I'd whisper into her ear. *"It's a Gift, Mamaw...we*

have to go!" And I'd take her hand and pull her towards
the door, giggling and squealing, tugging loose the bow of
her apron and letting it fall slow-motion to the floor
behind us, grabbing the keys, past Papaw laughing with
his pipe clamped between a few remaining teeth. Outside,
into the Rambler...gone, like clouds across blue, like pio-
neers...like sailors headed fearlessly towards the edge of
the earth...like children...

And this time, knowing just how beautiful getting lost can
be with a friend along, I wonder if we would consider
ever coming back.

≫◦≪

Ours was not a particularly artistic family. I never
dreamed of being on stage, at least not any stage outside
of my own imagination. Nothing could have seemed more
outrageous. But I suppose there were early indicators. At
one point I was somehow coerced into singing with the
children's choir at our church. We were dressed in our
white robes and brought in front of the congregation, and
though I remember little else about it one moment has
stayed with me. We had just finished singing something,
one of our very first performances, I suppose, and the little girl standing in front of me slowly turned and stared.
Her name was Nancy Taylor. We had played together
since we were toddlers, and she was one of my best
friends. But it was the first time she had really heard me
sing, I guess, and she turned from one step below me and
looked at me, her eyes wide, mouth slightly open.

"Jimmy *Robinson*!" she whispered. "You are going to be *famous* one day!" Everyone giggled, and my face flushed. I pretended to ignore her, but something in her words both startled and intrigued me. Now, I couldn't help wondering. I wondered what she had heard. I wondered if she could be right.

I didn't pursue singing at that point. But I did feel somehow drawn to the church—the feel of it, the smell of it, the musty warmth it provided. Once, as a teenager, when our church held the annual Youth Sunday, I was chosen to "preach" the sermon. Little memory remains of the undoubtedly horrific message I delivered, thank God, though I believe it was some revisionist travesty having to do with Matthew's "lilies of the field." I do remember feeling terribly nervous sitting there in the preacher's chair, a great throne-like thing of dark wood and red plush, but when they called my name I rose up in some fog of false confidence, and strode back and forth as I spoke, occasionally waving my arms, just as I'd seen our preacher do. It felt good, playing this new role. Once transformed into someone else, I felt more in control.

Later, having a celebration lunch at Frank's Catfish Cafe, my family praised me. My father said proudly, "It's like you'd been doing it your whole life." He looked somewhat amazed, as did everyone else. I never preached again, though. I had tried it, done it, and somehow that was enough. The initial rush was replaced by a hollow disappointment, not unlike the maiden voyage of my go-kart. In a way I could not explain, it all just seemed too easy. And all of the compliments, as badly as I longed to hear them, left me strangely unsatisfied. In my heart, I felt too much an imposter to deserve their praise.

Books were one of the few things that fed me; their words provided real sustenance. One of the most meaningful memories of my early education has to do with a black, tattered literature book in my grade school English class, a compilation of many English and American writers, with little thumbnail sketches of the authors above each piece. That started it. The love affair ignited. I buried my nose in their worlds and my head in their clouds, leaving the teacher and the rest of my class behind in that chalk-dusty old room, their voices becoming little more than a faint, surreal murmur—Keats and Shelley, Dickens and Poe, Hemingway and Frost and Sherwood Anderson, O. Henry and Welty and H. G. Wells, Browning and Dickinson and Shakespeare, and modern science fiction, too, stuff by Bradbury and Heinlein and Asimov. Off into their far-away places I flew, worlds filled with amazing adventures that made my town seem almost nonexistent. And from those moments, for as long as I can remember, I dreamed of being a writer.

I created my own stories, writing them in a spiral notebook, imitating the styles of my favorite authors, trying my best to *be* them. Putting my thoughts and feelings into words came easily to me, and had a therapeutic effect, but I always did so secretively, knowing the other guys would laugh at me if they knew. I loved creating other worlds, sometimes safe and sometimes scary worlds, places I could go any time I wanted to escape.

Still, I was just a boy, in love with doing the things boys love to do, so that my literary aspirations shared space and time with things like running wild and barefoot early on, football a little later, and girls a bit later still. My love for language never left me, though, and eventually I would find what seemed the perfect outlet for it.

❧❧

Mary Jo—1947
It's a studio photograph. There's a light reflecting off her curly hair, and she seems to be glowing. The prettiest thing, flashing that perfect smile. She's staring right at the camera, as if there's nothing in the whole world to be afraid of...

When young, my mother collected photographs and newspaper clippings and other things important to her, and glued them into a scrapbook. Of all the things in the box, this is the most difficult to finally touch, to feel, to fearfully open. The pages are brown and worn. But I find myself smiling, a little.

In it are wonderful pictures of her, blond and young and shining. There are several articles cut from local newspapers—1941, sixteen years old and a student at Murray High, a participant in an annual district music festival, listed as: "Soprano solo, 'Morning' by Speaks, Mary Jo Pentecost." And later, she's twenty, in a photo taken with five other young beauties, and beneath it reads—"Some of the prettiest talent in the Follies of 1945." In another article she's noted for winning a "Superior" prize in a state contest, and though I have no idea what that meant, she was clearly a fine singer, and loved to perform. My mother unknowingly helped set fire to something similar within me. Her music was to be a special gift, one that would shape much of my life to come.

My mother was like lightning. Both wonderful and fearful to watch, hers was an electric presence, leaping from one object to the next, perpetually charged and charging things. Her laughter burst out of her as if joy had jumped from behind something and shocked her, and tears could come with such shameless abandon that everyone near would be swept under. She loved her children in a breathless, desperate sort of way, as though from the moment we were born she began to fear losing us. Possessive and caring, volatile and scary, she was filled to overflowing with a life force that seemed almost too much for her to hold, sometimes violently shaking her from the inside, trying to get out. As quick to box my ear as to kiss my cheek, she shone like a wonderful sun-filled afternoon in the south, the kind that can with the slightest shift in the wind become ominously dark and send you running for cover. Throughout her life the storm would never subside, and the dizzy, light-headed roller coaster ride of loving her remains with me still.

Her hopes of one day becoming a professional performer never materialized. But I always thought of her as a sort of celebrity, a kind of undiscovered star. I could sense that God had gifted her, and had filled her with dreams. I would sit beside her in our little church and listen to her lilting soprano, marveling at its creamy, curling sound, a thin and sweet-swirling thing more angel than human, and I thought she was most fabulous indeed. *Near the cross, a trembling soul, love and mercy found me*—she sang, her voice cutting through and floating high above the creaking pews and the groaning, hissing radiators—*There the bright and morning star sheds its beams around me*...And how breathtakingly beautiful she was, her graceful neck white and arched, the words soaring through me both meaningless and magical, as I sat still and small and awed by the wonder of it all...*In the cross, in the cross, be my glory ever / Till my raptured soul shall find / Rest beyond the river...*

Barely five-foot-two, she could be heard (singing or yelling) for what seemed to me then like hundreds of miles. For a short but notorious period, when I was just old enough to both undress myself and to run very fast, I would be overcome by the boy in me, by the summer in me, I suppose, and as Mom stood at the kitchen window preparing supper, our phone would ring. "Mary Jo?"—a neighbors panicky voice—"You'd better look outside! Little Jimmy's runnin' through the neighborhood *nekkid* again!" And my mother would scream at my father, wailing like a siren through all of Benton County, "JIM! GO OUTSIDE AND GET YOUR NEKKID SON BACK IN THIS HOUSE!"

Seemingly always in movement, she was vibrant and alive and always flushed with something I can only call *life*—exciting and perplexing and marvelous and unpredictable. When angry she fearlessly attacked, clueless as a miniature poodle facing down a rottweiler. And yet there was something about her that always seemed breakable, and deep down I forever feared she might shatter, like porcelain, or be crushed, like a bird held too tightly.

Sometimes her music turned to something else, changing her. Red-faced and furious, she could fly in on me like a wildcat, swatting and slapping, terrible to behold. Then, moments later, the fire in her eyes softening, she would hold me close and shed tears along with mine, cuddling, cooing like a dove, my sweetheart once more.

Since we never knew who our mother was going to be, we children hadn't the slightest idea of who we were, either. It seemed as though I was never the same person. A wonderful child one moment, precious and cherished and loved beyond measure—*Come here, Sweetie...Momma's gotcha, my darling little boy*—and then, sometimes because of something I had done and often for no apparent reason at all, I would suddenly transform into someone vile and worthless, even hated. Her words cut through me then, like razors into my heart. I believed everything she said, of course, because she was my mother, and I loved her deeply, achingly, from down in my very soul. And so I knew I was loved, that I was special, and I also knew that with a flash of her all-knowing eyes I could change into a monster, becoming something hideous and hateful.

My sisters and I didn't know anything about depression or addiction or emotional illness, of course. We only knew that we loved her, and needed her, and depended on her in a way greater even than the way we depended on essential things like air and water and food. We rode the roller coaster with her, ever trusting. We existed in an often wonderful, sometimes fear-filled place, a never-knowing kind of place, unable to trust ourselves or anyone else, groping day after day through a schizophrenic world of obsession and rejection, needing her, constantly clinging to and cringing from, always running into her arms one moment and fleeing them the next.

Remembering. One day, when I was very young, something happened. I heard a sound in our house, one I had never heard before, faint and far away. Drawn against my will, the sound led me to her bedroom door. I felt very afraid, and wanted to call out to her, but could not. Slowly, I pushed open the door and looked into the room. My mother was bent over in a chair, crying; not the sad cry I had heard before in our home, but a deeper sound, awful and anguished, as if she were dying and in some unspeakable pain. The room felt very cold. She had not seen me yet, and still I could not speak. I reached out to her, silently, hesitantly, some huge and horrible thing beginning to clutch at my heart and tighten in my throat. Sadness filled me, and fear, so that tears flowed out of me as I perhaps for the first time realized with crushing clarity how suddenly she could be hurt, how easily she could be broken, how vulnerable...how *human* she was.

She looked up. The look on my face must have startled her, and brought her back to reality, because she stopped crying almost at once and held out her arms, letting me fall my last few steps into them. I pressed my face into her and took deep, sobbing breaths of White Shoulders, her favorite perfume. "It's alright, baby," she soothed. "Momma's alright, Momma's okay, don't cry baby..."

After that experience there was always some part of me more acutely aware of her fragility, and a more grownup kind of reality set in. I felt, perhaps, that I had suddenly taken on a new responsibility in my life, and that even though I was very young and very small it would from then on be my job to look after her, to watch over her. And I remember worrying about her. All the time.

I had no idea back then, and have only recently begun to grasp the truth of it, but I believe my mother was one of those creatures designed by God to *shine*, to give all of herself, born for flight yet both thrilled and terrified by the flying, and destined for something other than a soft and easy landing. I don't know what happened to her dreams, whatever they might have been. I'm not sure if marriage and children interrupted her hopes of something else. But looking back at her now from this distance, I don't believe she ever felt quite satisfied with her life, as if somewhere in her secret heart she sensed that she had been made for other things, other faraway places, living out dreams that were simply too big for our little town to hold. I will never know the truth, I suppose, but for a while at least she burned brightly, though her audience was small. She seemed destined to dazzle, to entertain, to wow us like fireworks, *like lightning*. Beautiful. Frightening. Brief.

The place where I went to high school was called Camden Central High, and in this building, in the creaky old gymnasium, two very important events in my life were to occur. The first happened when I was around six or seven years old. My mother was one of two women who organized the

Quarterback Club Talent Show, a local fundraiser for the football team. This event always produced a grab bag of entertainment ranging from the hopelessly awful to the mildly amusing. Looking back, I think this was possibly the happiest I ever saw my mother, a young woman in her natural habitat, beaming and strutting and soaking up every precious moment in the spotlight, small spotlight that it may have been.

There are a couple of moments in that evening that have never left me. I remember the night, and the breathless anticipation of *Show Business*! And somehow, to this little kid sitting out there in the audience in front of the stage with the lights turned off in the gym and the PA system blaring and the electric hum of all these local town-folk starved for entertainment, there came an instinctive knowing that something wonderful was about to happen.

After an assortment of funny-bad skits and pathetic attempts at magic tricks and singing that would make a hound dog run for cover, a fellow named Steve Joyner came on stage. He was an older guy, a real musician who played in a local "combo." He walked on stage carrying this amazing, shiny black electric guitar and proceeded to play along with a scratchy recording of "Memphis." My jaw dropped. Everything else going on around me and inside of me instantaneously ceased to exist. The sound that started with his fingers and blared through the amp burned a place of permanent residence into my brain.

For about four minutes, I did not breathe. My life was changed forever. *To be able to do that*—I thought then—

would be better than anything. Better than flying like an eagle, better than hitting home runs, better than being Captain America. It was far and away the coolest thing I had ever seen or heard, and in many ways I haven't gotten over it yet.

Then came the grand finale, a duet featuring my mother and her friend and co-organizer of the show. I'm not sure what song they sang. It might have been "Jack The Knife" or maybe "Ballin' the Jack." And I really couldn't tell you now if they were, on a professional level, any good or not. But as I sat perched on my knees in that metal folding chair, wide-eyed and gape-mouthed like some hypnotized chipmunk, I witnessed something I can never forget, and felt a feeling I have been actively seeking to reproduce for most of my life since. I saw my mother singing and dancing, her pretty legs kicking high in dance shoes and stockings, her face painted and glorious, lips red as apples, eyes like Fourth of July sparklers. I witnessed her channeling something remarkable, something otherworldly, something *Godly.* Flowing out of her came whole joy, a sort of fulfilled completeness, and up there on that stage with the colored lights shining down on her I saw something in her face that I had never before seen. Coming from a place much deeper down than where things usually come from, *I saw her soul smile.*

Inspired, I went home and immediately began lobbying my parents for a guitar. That Christmas my wish came true, though instead of shiny black wood and metal it was small and brown and mostly plastic. I thought it incredibly beautiful. To sweeten the deal my parents had arranged for Steve Joyner *himself* to give me lessons. And though this would be a perfect spot in the script to launch my story about the inevitable and successful musical career, for whatever reasons the guitar lessons never stuck. I think I was too awestruck by my instructor to pay attention to the instruction. Eventually, I put the guitar in the closet and the idea of stardom out of my mind. I allowed the dream to fade. At least for a while.

Probably, it was because of girls. Falling in love became my number one preoccupation. There was little red-haired Kathy, my first kiss, the two of us pressing our lips together in an awkward and extraordinarily long moment, a breath-defying, life-affirming moment, one I have of course never forgotten. When I hit my teens there was Dianne, dark-haired and exotic-looking compared to the blond females in my family, a real farmer's daughter with a wild flash in her black eyes and the intoxicating smell of wind in her hair and fresh corn and spring onions on her breath. Later, when just old enough to fall but still too young to know better, it would be Carrie, the new Presbyterian preacher's daughter. She, too, was dark-haired and appropriately mysterious, though her skin was porcelain-pretty and pale as moonlight. Her eyes shone sad and round, the color of molasses, and I was helpless from the first moment I looked into them. Ours was a young romance that nearly killed us both, a thing tortur-ous and too old for us, a sort of brutally beautiful and naïve passion always quivering between us, the kind of intensely innocent union that in a few swift seasons causes hearts to prematurely grow up, and then breaks them.

Later, it would end, with appropriate teen angst. Although I knew within me that she was all I would ever want or need, I assumed she would wait for me always as I went selfishly into college, in pursuit of new adventure. And so, although we both vainly tried to make it last beyond high school, I had by then already promised my young heart and soul to something else. And our world—barely—never happened.

I found my own gift for music at a relatively late age. I was nearly seventeen before it occurred to me that I might have any talent for it at all, and by then, ensconced in my role as football-playing-one-of-the-guys, I was embarrassed to admit what was happening. In those days, in my town at least, being a rock musician was not the somewhat commonplace dream that it would later become. One was considered a bit odd, if not completely deviant, to grow long hair and jump around on a stage in front of people. To many in our community it meant dope-smoking, flag-burning, hippie-loving *trouble*. The very few kids who seemed interested in that sort of thing were not generally thought of as "good" kids. Most of my friends at that time, I believed, might have thought I'd gone weird on them had they discovered what was happening inside me, and at first I told virtually no one. It was one thing to *listen* to rock-and-roll, but another thing altogether to consider *playing* it.

One night, I woke from one dream into another. I kept a small radio under my pillow, tuned to an FM station in Memphis, and I would fall asleep listening. My parents did not know this. The signal came and went, but on some nights it was clear and strong. And on this night I felt myself slipping out of sleep, as if being gently but irresistibly summoned by a voice, and half-awake I became aware of something miraculous happening inside me. From very far away—sounds, and voices, and some power surging through me, a pulse, completely transforming. I became so entranced that I didn't know or care if I was dreaming or not. *Na na na, na-na-na-na...*a foreign language I understood perfectly, persuasive and powerful, changing me. My heart pounded. I was scared to move, not wanting to frighten the spirit away, this raspy, repeating phrase coming from a two-inch speaker through my feather pillow. Slowly, I heard some words mixed in with the distant magic, over and over again, *na-na-na-naa, Hey Jude...*

The next morning, even though daylight had returned, all my senses had not. I knew, then, that music could be a mystical thing, whether the one making the music was aware of it or not. I now understood song as an extraordinary and potentially Divine force, knowing that sometimes even when the words appeared on the surface meaningless, they nonetheless held the potential for great power.

I had discovered the rush that could transport me anywhere. My dad bought me a stereo system for my birthday, and I sat in my bedroom listening for hours, awed, concentrating, scanning the lyrics and absorbing the feel of it all. I played the music loud enough so that it drowned out all the other sounds in the house, the unnerving sounds, or the uneasy silence in between. I loved my music, and my room. I felt safe in there.

Ultimately, though, listening wasn't enough. Despite the irrationality of it, against all logic and reason, I felt drawn out of my safe sanctuary. I knew my becoming a musician wasn't possible. But something kept pulling at me, tugging at the unbeliever within, until almost against my will I found myself doing a very strange thing. I would wait until my parents and my sisters were all out of the house, and then, it being the only musical instrument available, I would sneak down into the living room and sit at the piano. A spinet piano, one my parents had purchased so that my two sisters could take lessons. Everyone did it back then, apparently; you bought a piano and when the female children reached a certain age, you paid someone to give them music lessons. (My sisters took these lessons for years, and neither of them can play a note today). And so there it sat, mostly untouched. Though I had little idea how the thing worked, I knew that it was somehow capable of producing music. In reality, I would have preferred playing electric guitar, slung low and dangerous, like Billy Gibbons or Jimmy Page or Joe Walsh. But the piano was the only instrument in the house, my plastic guitar having been long since stomped on and discarded. And, after all, Elton John and Billy Joel played piano. And so, my unlikely journey began.

Jimmy's Band—The Sunrise Collection—1972
Me and my four buddies, standing together in my living room. Behind us, there's a set of orange

drums set up in the corner, and a small guitar amp. We're all laughing, as if we share some hysterical secret. As if we're never going to stop...

I started one finger at a time. It was the most unlikely of things; I couldn't read or write music, and had absolutely no idea what I was doing, but clearly God had poured the gift into me, and once I dared open the bottle the stuff poured out. There was something fascinating about it. By simply pressing down a key, I could summon a clear, pure note. I could make the note do different things. I could make it soft or loud, like a tiny bird or a clap of thunder. I could add certain other notes and create even richer tones, sounds that bled together, meshed, became another and very separate thing, almost alive. It seemed to me quite wondrous, this ability to control sound, and with it color and emotion and texture above and apart from myself. Entranced, I hunched over the piano for as long as the house was empty, prodding emotion from the keys, transfixed. Almost from the very first, it had little to do with me. I seemed to be channeling something. A seed apparently planted in me at the beginning of time was now breaking through the surface.

Soon I added more fingers, and before long I was "playing by ear" and writing my own little melodies and words. This went on for some time as a clandestine sort of thing, my advancement considerably stymied by the infrequency of an empty house for my "sessions." But something began to happen, and has not stopped happening to this day. I found out a secret, one from within me, one that I did not know existed. I discovered, almost by chance, that I could sing my heart better than I could speak it.

≈≈≈

"Mom," I said. "I want you to hear something." She stood in the next room, at the kitchen sink, an apron around her waist. She and I were the only ones home. I had been waiting for one of her "good" days. Today she was up and about, dressed, her hair and makeup done, smiling, doing things. Over the sound of running water I could hear her singing softly. The entire house was taking a deep, thankful breath. The sun shone.

"What is it?" she called. I closed my eyes.

"It's important, Mom," I said, resolute. She—none of them—had any idea. It had taken me months to work up the courage. As if sensing something in my voice, she came through the door and stared at me, puzzled. I sat there stiffly on the piano bench, my hands hiding under my thighs.

"What?" she said, quietly. She looked at me wonderingly, as if half-expecting another of my silly jokes. And I took a breath and freed my hands, and I played and sang her some little song I had written. God only knows what it must have sounded like, but I didn't stop or look up from the keys until the end. And when it was finished, the last note held its breath and I held mine, until finally I had to look up at her.

She did not speak. She was smiling the strangest smile, a deeply pleased and baffled smile, looking at me as though we had never met and yet had never been closer, as if I was both a stranger and also some inseparable piece of her heart. It is one of the few times I had ever seen her at a loss for words. Something about her softened, and for a moment she looked more beautiful to me than ever. Even now I can see her face clearly, her hands slowly coming together under her chin, as if she were about to pray.

"That was...*wonderful*," she said.

That freed me. I performed for the whole family that night. I don't really recall the overall reaction, other than it being mostly positive. Dad seemed non-judgmental, thankfully, though slightly alarmed, as if he feared an alien life force had taken over his son's body. But he never said a discouraging word, and from then on I embraced it, this strange and out-of-nowhere gift. I was on my way. I felt that I had finally discovered a uniform that fit.

First, it had been Little League. Later, it was football. I had played all through junior high, my absurdly large shoulder pads coming up to my ears. My mother was terrified. I wasn't much more than half the size of every other kid playing. Yet I felt determined that destiny would one day crown me as rightful heir to Bullet Bob's crown, fastest man in the NFL. What I lacked in talent was temporarily compensated for by my fierce desire to be fearless.

As a freshman in high school, I stood 5'7" and weighed 137 pounds. The coaches thought I had *potential*.

I learned to use my small frame like a torpedo, flashing in from my defensive halfback position, sacrificing my body to bring down bigger guys by taking out their legs. By the time I was a junior in high school, I still stood 5'7" and still weighed 137 pounds. They tried everything. Health shakes. Banana splits. At one point, I think, someone considered beer, though the idea was eventually rejected. Nothing had any effect. I had stopped growing, while the rest of my teammates continued to add bulk and strength and speed. All of the stress resulting from running on my flat feet had caused tendonitis in both knees, and I was no longer Bullet Jimmy. My reckless torpedo tackles were leaving me banged up and the ball carriers unaffected. I began to dread the practices. The truth had become clear: I was never going to be big, and I was never going to be a star player. As dreams go, this one was turning out to be another dud.

But none of that really mattered now. I began to realize that girls, a subject I had most certainly been steadily *gaining* interest in, really kind of *liked* guys who played and sang music. So that, even though a few friends (and virtually all adults) viewed my apparent philosophical conversion with at best a sort of bemused skepticism, I gained new—and, I thought then, much *cooler*—cohorts, not to mention a new kind of admiration from the fairer sex as well. I had found my *destiny*.

The rest happened the way such things happen, I suppose. My new, musically-minded buddies and I formed a little band, though in our case we wrote our own songs and rarely played material written by other people. For a while we remained a somewhat secretive bunch, rehearsing at my house. But gradually we grew bolder, realizing we could never again live without this magical thing we'd found. In a few short months, we felt ready. Summoning all our courage, the decision was made, a decision that would change me forever.

And so, after practicing for about a year, a *second* thing happened in that same old gymnasium: A junior in high school now, at another talent show, only this time my friends and I are on the stage. I remember clearly my intense nervousness; I can only imagine how bad we must have been. But something happened that night. Despite all the odds against us, that gym grew almost eerily quiet as we began to play. I have no idea what song we performed, or what words I had written. But something came over nearly everyone in that gym, a force that froze them. The creaky old place suddenly fell still, and awkwardly silent. When our first song ended, the applause rolled down on us like ocean waves, spontaneous and sincere and loud. I felt something flow through me like warm syrup, and I began to glow, and to float, and to feel indescribably intoxicated. I finally felt it. At long last, *connected*.

I quit the football team, started wearing the hippy-est clothes my parents would allow, and became intensely interested in things "counter cultural." My band played high school dances and proms, lugging our amps and speakers into the National Guard Armory or the church fellowship hall. In a short period of time I went from steady, relatively well-adjusted small town boy to would-be Rock Star, longing for high school graduation so that I could grow my hair longer, do stronger drugs, and take my rightful place on the cover of *Rolling Stone*. Always a natural dreamer, this became my new dream. One that almost came true.

And so I began to grow out of my old clothes and out of my old dreams and into new ones. I began to confuse the stuff of God with the stuff of humankind, to interpret the God-Dreams as gifts of my own making. This would be an incredibly exciting and creative time, though in some ways the sky would never be the same blue again, the air never taste as sweet. Although within me the spirit of adventure still lived and the child remained enchanted, the dreams had begun moving into a new season, and everything and everyone else—Mamaw, my mother and father, my sisters, and my God—slowly started to fade, backstage, out of my spotlight.

This didn't happen all at once, of course, and in most ways I remained unaware of it happening at all. But little by little I began trying to take back and possess that which had never belonged to me in the first place. I began to think it was *me*, and that because of it I could control and manipulate the people and circumstances of my life in any way I chose. I would end up very, very lost, in a dark wood with nowhere left to turn, down a lonely dead-end road, desperately shouting out directions.

But by then, there was no one at the wheel.

the storm

Something was wrong with our home. From the earliest impressions made upon my mind and heart—as a toddler, perhaps, or even before—I believe I was if not cognizant then at least aware on some level that our family suffered from an obscure yet tangible brokenness. We were less than whole. Maybe we had always known it, at least in our hearts, though like all sick families we had little else to could go by. The truth—the truth we pretended wasn't real—was that something had been wrong for a very long time. We dwelled within walls of the only reality we had ever experienced, the only home we had ever known. We all learned to retreat, to move away from what should have been the center, running into our own imagined realities instead of each other's arms, isolated, cut off from one another and from ourselves. Maybe the delusional world in which we lived fooled most of us most of the time. Somewhere, though, deep down, we knew. Children know. And little by little the illusion began falling away. Our world began to slowly crumble, the once tightly tied rope began to loosen, and all the things I had depended on all my life began to unravel and fall away.

Looking back now I can see that no one was really at fault, though we all tried to blame someone or something at the time. We became a family lost in fear; my father, my sisters, all of us, confused and helpless, scattered rather than bonded, and huddled noiselessly in our separate rooms that had once made up a home. Something was happening to us, and none of us knew how to make it go away.

None of us now can say when it began, probably because it had always been a part of us, to some degree. Even when we were very young, she would startle us, changing before our eyes. We were always wondering, at any given moment, who she might become.

Apparently she talked about it often to friends, brooding, constantly questioning not *if* it would happen to her, but *when*. She had been forever fleeing from her mother's illness, and at least in some hidden part of herself had accepted emotional breakdown as her ultimate fate. At some point fear had become a sort of uneasy ally, a companion she walked alongside because she felt she must; it was who she was, and what she would no doubt become.

This confused my sisters and me. As children, we couldn't comprehend why she was not always the same person. She would shine so brightly one moment, and then the sparkle would fade into a blue blaze, the color of panic, like the eyes of an animal under attack. Her behavior, once spontaneous and exciting, grew increasingly frightening to us, and we knew that something was very wrong, but felt powerless to stop it.

It would be wrong to paint within our house a picture of constant doom and gloom. There were many happy times, especially early on. Our parents cared for us generously, and loved us deeply. As children, we had everything we wanted, and almost all we ever dreamed of. But although there was much laughter in our house, over time we learned to laugh too loud and too hard, a forced and futile kind of display, with a vague tone of desperation hidden in the sound. Still, laughter was far more desirable than the alternative, and I enthusiastically took upon myself the very serious role of Family Clown. It became my passionate desire to hear them all laugh, especially Momma. The high, life-giving sound of her happiness filled me with peace, if only temporarily.

On the good days, when a light seemed to come into the house, we all became blissful and free, emerging from hiding, celebrating, working ourselves into a frenzy, like dogs let loose after being too long penned up. So that, day after day, whether or not our home was covered by storm or by sunlight, we were never quite certain of how we were supposed to be feeling, or acting.

Over time, things worsened. By the time I started high school Momma had become more verbally abusive, always complaining, as if she felt everyone was trying to ruin her already miserable life. She wailed that none of us loved her any more, that we never wanted to spend time with her, and then cursed and screamed whenever we tried to draw near. "No one *loves* me!" she would moan, not letting us, then "LEAVE ME ALONE!" And we would.

By this time the prevailing wisdom of the medical community had begun prescribing drugs to make her feel happy when depressed, pills to make her sleep, pills to wake her up, the vicious cycle begun. She was drinking by then, too, though we went along as if we didn't know. We longed for her, yet we no longer recognized her, and the more she changed the more we retreated. And longed for her still.

At times, life was almost comical. Or at least that's what we pretended. Once, in the middle of the night during a thunderstorm, Momma woke all of us and—with my father's somewhat silent support—herded us from the upstairs bedrooms down into the living room. The power was out, and Dad wielded a flashlight.

"Everybody on the couch!" she ordered, voice quavering, her face white. "Take your feet off the floor!" And we did, complaining but obedient, knowing it was foolish and yet too frightened not to obey. She had often told us how her own mother had been terrified of storms, making her sit away from the windows when she was a little girl, feet tucked beneath her, safe from the deadly electricity that would surely flow through the floor each time the lightning struck. I moaned and feigned unconcern, stealing glances at my family each time the lightning illuminated a brief, flashing glimpse of their faces...huddled there in our helpless circle like war victims during a bombing raid...my older sister, knees pulled under her chin, with, what—embarrassment? Anger? Jennifer, shivering, cringing with each clap of thunder, learning the fear...my father, stone-faced, acquiescent. But mostly I watched my mother, this poor creature sitting cross-legged on a footstool, the white of her eyes showing, entangling her hands and jumping like a little lost girl every time the sky lit up and the rumbles shook the windows. The storm outside didn't frighten me. But I could see clearly the one raging within her, and I prayed desperately for it to blow away.

Mornings at the breakfast table had become torturous, a sort of cereal-bowl insurrection at which my sisters and father and I tried mostly to avoid the embarrassing pain of it all and just get away to work and school. My sisters and I knew, too, that by then there was little love left between our parents. Perhaps the bond had been long broken, or maybe my father had slowly lost his love for her as she lost herself, but we knew the truth in that sure way children know such things, and it shattered us. Never a very communicative family, and with no real faith as a place of refuge, we took cover and ducked behind the temporary shelter of our own minds, hoping the storm would pass and the laughter return. But, for the most part, it never did.

We all shared in the helplessness, sitting by our own windows, watching the sky, counting the seconds between flashes, calculating the distance of the storm. We blamed each other, I suppose, because there was no one else to blame, and of course we each mostly blamed ourselves.

My father grew more withdrawn, always trying to shield the children, perhaps, and himself, unwittingly teaching us that feelings couldn't hurt us if we kept them at a distance, secret and hidden. Still, I wanted him to save us, to somehow put a stop to the madness. We sat at supper, staring at our plates, withered by the barrage of hateful, shaming words, so that after a while we couldn't really hear them anymore. Slump-shouldered, wilted under the weight of it all, we tensed our legs, waiting to run.

I tuned out my mother's voice, and waited for Dad to rescue us. Day after day, night after night, he would sit and eat, the fork mechanically moving to his mouth, chewing, silent except for a low, nearly inaudible groan sneaking out each time he exhaled. I sat nearest him, and I could hear it, could see him out of the corner of my eye—forkful of food into his mouth, the muscles in his jaw working, clinching, and then the little groans. I couldn't understand it. We were the children, and we had been taught not to speak. And so I waited. I knew the day would come; he was only preparing for the right moment. He would stand up one morning from behind his bacon and eggs and let loose a retaliatory strike, powerful and commanding, words of authority that would somehow break Mom out of the evil spell she was under and return our home to sanity. He would do it, someday. I just knew it.

Say something.

Silently, pleading.

Tell her to stop. Make all this go away...

Our house was hushed, numbed by her ravings. Stealing a glance at my father, I could see his jaw working, his face impassive, blank.

Please make it stop...Please God, save us.

Remembering. Four of us in the car together, Mom and Dad in the front seat, Jennifer and me in back. I'm eleven, maybe twelve. Sitting in the parking lot at the community pool, waiting for Joette to stop talking with her teenage friends so we could go home. We'd been joking about how long it was taking her to get in the car. And I said something, repeated something I'd heard my mother say countless times. Kidding around, thinking it would be funny, I guess, maybe even make Momma laugh a little—a phrase she would use, almost but not quite casually, anytime someone was behaving in a way that didn't suit her. She hated her mother, I think, at least the mad part of her, the part always ringing in her ears, that relentless voice the two of them shared. And she loved her deeply, of course, and so suffered within this conflict, always longing for life without her, secretly wishing to be rid of her, but knowing she might somehow perish the moment they separated. Her conversations were littered with "Big Mama-isms." And so, on this day, as all of us were kidding about Joette being somewhat scatter-brained, I forced a laugh and repeated one of my mother's favorites—"Lordy, she's worse than Big Momma." Out of the corner of my eye, I saw Mom twisting her body around, and then she struck, a half-slap, half-fist to the side of my face, knocking my head into the window. I saw sparks behind my eyelids. The car fell silent. *The taste of blood in my mouth.* I opened my eyes to see if she was going to hit me again. And when our eyes met, *I knew she was not there.*

At that moment I felt much more afraid than hurt, afraid of what I saw and what I didn't see. It wasn't the fact that she had hit me; she had hit me before. It was her eyes. They looked through me, unaware of me. Only for a moment, but long enough. The eyes flashed black and empty with a fury that sucked the soul from me. I saw no trace of love in them at all. I had pushed a button, and my mother disappeared. She didn't strike again, but sat glaring at me for another moment, then turned back around, talking to herself, cursing, her voice low and guttural, unrecognizable. And then I felt something like intense anger, a blinding blackness, an almost uncontrollable desire to let loose my outrage—*I will not cry, I will NOT CRY*—gritting my teeth, ashamed of the tears falling defiantly onto my shirt, silently convulsing, the murderous screams banging around my insides, hating my cowardice, hating myself. I wanted to run, but didn't. I wanted someone to say something, to save me. But there was only silence.

My father sat very still, tensed, staring straight ahead through the windshield, his hands at 10 and 2.

Joette was older, and perhaps understood a little better than her two younger siblings, though that probably made it worse in some ways. Jennifer was the youngest, and the most tender-hearted by nature, and would take more of the brunt of our mother's attack since she would ultimately be at home the longest—the raging, the demoralizing barrage of hateful words, the daily attempts to fill us with guilt for abandoning her, even as she unwittingly pushed us away.

"What's wrong with Momma?" my little sister asked one day, as if she had just been made aware of some long-hidden secret. Momma had screamed at her, chasing her through the house, slapping at her, and Jennifer ducked into my room for sanctuary. She had always been the gentlest one, soft in spirit, easy to make smile or to hurt, and lonely somehow. I tried to protect her when we were little. Always the quiet one, her question startled me, and startles me still.

"Nothing," I muttered, or something equally evasive, and tried to ignore her, to ignore everything. I just went on about whatever I was doing, pretending, fantasizing. *Nothing's happening, nothing's wrong, just leave it alone.* We had stopped talking very much by now. How desperately we needed each other, and how hard we tried to pretend that we didn't.

I won't try to explain what happened to our mother. I more often than not see only dusty, empty rooms when I go in search for her back there, to that place of my past where my mind sometimes wanders but rarely lingers. I believe in words like psychosis and bipolar disease and schizophrenia, and I believe in chemical imbalances and "bad wiring" of the brain. I can spout lots of technical jargon and use psychoanalytical language to describe some things science understands and some things it does not. I'm supposed to have some understanding of neurotransmitters and receptor molecules, but all that cannot completely explain how people sometimes become lost to themselves and lost to the rest of us. And I believe in unseen darkness and demons, too, and I'm not at all sure where one set of beliefs leaves off and the other takes up. All I know for sure is that God exists, that there is a world beyond what we can see and touch and feel, and that within that world evil exists, too. And I believe that for some of us in obvious ways and probably all of us in more subtle ways the disease exists and makes its home in more than just our flesh, and medicine alone rarely cures us. When all my training fails me, sometimes all I really know for sure is that being well—truly well—goes to a place within us that lies far deeper than the mere molecules that make us up, and that for reasons known and unknown our mother began to fall away from us. Isolated, abandoned, sitting for hours in that same room where we had so often been saved from the lightning, she stared out at the intruding gray, grieving, mourning something lost that none of us could help her find.

I wanted to sit with her and hold her, but couldn't bear it all, somehow, and so I hid my heart and passed quickly by her doorway, longing to touch her, praying she would not notice me and call out my name, slipping silently up to my room, where I would softly close the door between me and the deepening dusk of her far-away pain.

I do remember Dad taking us to visit her at the "hospital" in Memphis. She was supposed to be "resting." But we knew this was not an ordinary hospital. She had been gone for what seems like forever, though it was only a few weeks. And I seem to recall some fragment of memory, overhearing someone talk about "shock treatments." The words held no specific meaning for me, yet they were spoken in hushed and serious tones that filled me with a crushing sadness, and something like helpless, hopeless rage.

I can still smell the place, can still *feel* it...that long hall of wheelchairs and soft shuffling slippers, absent faces, tortured faces, faces blissfully unaware...distant moans and low cries for help, a big room with lots of barred windows, and faces staring out at the sky as if they barely recognized it. And then she was there, led by a nurse from her room into this unlikely place, slowly, as if walking in her sleep. I can see Momma in a white robe, her hair brushed back in a strange way, as if someone else had done it for her, her face painted into a smile that wasn't quite a real smile, not *her* smile, the lipstick too red and smudged at one corner, her speech slurred. And a strange silence falling over us—the charade collapsing as we hugged her, tears in her eyes and then in ours, a cold-knife sadness none of us fully understood cruelly wedging itself between us. She was a stranger, this crushed and pitiful little woman pretending to be well, and we were all awkward and numb and silent, caught there in an impossible horror, helpless against the overwhelming sense of losing her, even as we held on tight. And even now, perhaps *especially* now, I can't stare at that place for long without turning away my eyes.

Strange, the things we remember, and the things we forget. I don't recall much in the way of a time-line for it all, and interestingly enough neither does the rest of my family. It is a time shoved aside, swept into the corner, nothing more than a bad dream best forgotten but never quite gone. It's not easy finding my way back. I can find few photographs, no roadmaps, as though there was a missing period of our lives, like a collective blackout. I go back blindly, and ask a lot of questions. I ask my father, and my sisters. Questions about names, dates, circumstances, but mostly about feelings.

"How was it for you?" I ask Joette. We're having dinner together at my house. "How did you feel?" She looks at me, and blinks. In her fifties now, divorced, still vibrant and quick to laugh, positive and energetic despite a battle with lupus. I try again—"How old were you when you first noticed things changing with Mom?"—or something like that. And her answers are always brief, guarded by the little bursts of laughter, as though going back there now seems unnecessary, as though pausing too long to think about it might accidentally unearth something best left buried.

"I really can't say," softly, pushing the food around her plate with a fork. "It was hard, I remember that." And I ask for specifics, and she is unable or unwilling to supply them. "I dunno," she says. "I was thirteen or fourteen, maybe," or "It was the early sixties" or "Maybe Daddy or Jennifer might know." And it is only after I leave it alone for a few minutes that she finally chooses to remember something, and tells me in the most casual of tones about the time she was a sophomore in high school, and how she and her best friend had been in a car one afternoon with their two boyfriends...*A thunderstorm is blowing in, and even though Joette knows how terrified Mom will be, she and her friends decide to drive to the park. They sit there in the car for a while, watching the storm, laughing, smooching, being young. But when she finally gets home, Mom meets her at the door, and without warning begins to grab and claw and slap her, dragging my sister into a corner and beating her down, cursing, tiny white specks of spit flying from her mouth, with me and my father and my little sister and even another married couple standing there watching, apparently too stunned to intervene. Finally, her rage exhausted, Mom lets up and Joette escapes, her face red and puffy, shame and anger and tears all over her as she runs past us and out of the room...*

I had no memory of the event at all, until my sister told me. And then, a door unlocks, and creaks open, breaking through the cobwebs into a damp and stale room long abandoned. And over the next few days following our dinner together I *did* see it, and other things, too, in brief but vivid flashes, faces seen just for an instant, as if lit up by lightning in a darkened room, things that made me wince—the blind rage of it, the horror of it—things too awful for a child to see, and too awful to remember. And with these images comes some sense of other times—more violence, physical and verbal, things broken and never put back together, the emotional body parts of our family still scattered about, unattended to, never faced, never washed, and never healed.

And even now, trying to go back and stare at things long avoided, attempting to paint a clear picture with only a box of old photographs to go by, even now I wonder how many more things are still lost, faded and just out of frame, put away in a nailed-shut cellar somewhere inside me, these things we forget.

And maybe the details don't matter as much as we think. Because for whatever reason and perhaps for no reason at all, our mother became ill. Her life changed, and ours with it. I'm not sure when it started or how quickly it worsened. It was, in a way, like the slow closing of a morning glory at dusk. She began to lose her light, and we all watched her fold into a darkness that would eventually cause her to wither and never open again.

We ran. I dug deeper into my bedroom, my stereo, my books, my band. The rest of my family ran, too, in their own separate directions, and in their own separate ways. Somehow we turned to everything but *Him,* the one who could have saved us.

Maybe we—all of us, all of His children—never really know how hurt we are. Maybe some of us are weaker than others, or somehow more vulnerable, while some of us steel ourselves against this thing called life and hide behind something very false that we call "strength." And all of us—the weak and the willful, the imposters and the heroes—we each find some way to stuff it all down into different places and deal with it in different ways, to pretend that it's killing us or that it doesn't hurt at all, to give it too much power or not enough and either way become its victim. Perhaps some of us go through our entire lives accepting pain as a normal part of the process, while others can never quite stop the bleeding, never fully heal, and in some strange way become almost passionately attached to the wound, embracing it and nurturing it until finally it becomes an essential part of who we are.

What I was to become can certainly not be blamed on anyone or anything other than myself. What happened to me was not anyone else's fault—certainly not my parents, who tried to love me the best they could, always giving me as much of themselves as they knew how. I can't blame them any more than they could have blamed their own parents, or their own circumstances. Maybe I had my own "bad wiring," and what happened to me would have taken place regardless of what went on around me. I don't know. I may never know.

And, probably, knowing wouldn't have changed a thing.

the thirst

I can wonder about these things now, though I could not—or *did* not—back then. I had my first real job, working at the Eva Road Grocery, a little bait and beer stop between town and the river. I worked there summer afternoons, stocking groceries, pumping gas, letting the silver minnows slip between my fingers as I counted them from the gurgling bait tanks into the fishermen's buckets. Later, my junior year in high school, I landed the coolest job in town, working the counter at Billy Fry's Rexall Drug Store. They were good days, in many ways.

Mostly, though, I just wanted to run away. At seventeen, I had big plans. I couldn't ditch that cornball hick town fast enough to suit me, especially now that I'd discovered rock-and-roll, marijuana, and free love (or at least the promise of it). I can't remember exactly where we were or who was performing at the time, but in a nearby city with some friends, sitting at an outdoor concert with the night air suspended on electricity and lights and dope smoke, I had a vision: Staring at the stage full of musicians, then leaning back on the grass and gazing into the stars, I knew what I wanted to do, what I wanted to *be*. And from that moment on, for what seemed a very long time, my little hometown lost its hold on my heart.

I began to change. And yet I didn't really *feel* changed. I was not yet heartless. There were sharp pangs of sadness, somewhere in me, whenever I heard Suzie barking at the back door, standing there for hours after I'd come home from school. Her whining was sad and insistent. But I was too busy; there was a room to hide in, music to turn up loud, girls to call. I avoided going into the kitchen, where she could see me through the storm door. I couldn't bear to see her face, now streaked with gray on the muzzle, staring in at me, deeply puzzled, eyes forlorn. Her neglected and matted tail never stopped wagging, determinedly optimistic, forever young. There was still something very young inside of me, too, a part of me that would sometimes be filled with a kind of regret and remorse, sending me out to sit with her a while, rubbing her ears. But hurting was something I was determined not to feel, and learning to ignore. Turning my back on her was, barely, less painful than looking into her face. I rarely spared more than a few minutes before going back into the house, to other and more grown up things. Suzie would then resume her pleas, not giving up until the sun went down.

I never felt that I had fallen out of love with my family, with running through the woods beside my dog, or with summer and sneakers and creeks and high grass. I didn't wake one morning with a plan. I never said to Mamaw—*I'm too old for our games. I want to play Getting Lost by myself from now on.* But she felt it. How sad it must have made her, this silent drifting away of her friend. Of course, she had always known I would grow up, had been praying for it every day, and was I'm sure very proud watching it happen. Still, we never discussed it, this bittersweet changing of things, and perhaps children never do. I can't really remember telling her goodbye. But of all the old pains that now sometimes rise within me, right in the middle of any ordinary day, and strike me in some tender place not quite healed, this one draws the most blood. I want to see her. I want to tell her that I know how selfish I was, and how sorry I am that we missed even one more moment together.

One day, Suzie wasn't there to meet me when I got home from school. Nearly fifteen years old now, she was slow to get up in the morning, and limping badly by the end of the day. My father had mentioned having her put to sleep, but the rest of the family pretended not to hear him, and nothing was ever done. On this day, the yard seemed strangely silent, and vacant. I called her, but she never came.

I'm not sure how I found out. Maybe Dad told me, or maybe he didn't have to. I never asked. I felt cheated, and abandoned, and hollow. But it was the way of things by now. We never discussed it. No one asked, and no one told. We all lived out the days as if on separate worlds. We did not share our secrets. I had a few fleeting fantasies of rushing home from school, of saving my dog before they carried her away, just in the nick of time. But then I pushed them out of my mind, and closed the door. I never acknowledged the loss, or grieved.

I went to bed that night, too grown up to cry.

I wanted out. Maybe a lot of this is only natural. Perhaps God puts us together this way, so that as a boy becomes a man something calls out to him and draws him away from where he is towards what he might become. But my desire was tainted. I felt bored with everything around me. I desperately wanted something. A need burned in me, and began shaping and compelling me, and ultimately distancing me.

The boy slowed. He stopped running and laughing, a little at a time, and he became bored with the woods and the stars and the bugs and the wind blowing clear water from his eyes as he flew through space on his bike, and he stopped spinning with his arms spread out like a helicopter and rolling down hills like a fallen tree and swinging like Tarzan from a rope swing tied to heaven, until finally there was no more innocent sleep at the end of a perfect day, head pressed into the womb of his pillow, listening for the very heartbeat of God. And from then on, no matter how hard he tried, *the boy could never get enough.*

I stopped talking to my Friend. Over time, I began speaking to Him with just my head instead of my heart, an increasingly disinterested and one-sided conversation, then eventually not at all. Somehow we grew apart, as friends often do. I don't know why. Maybe my other friends, the ones of flesh and blood, clamored for my attention, and the noises of "reality" drowned out the whispers of His presence. For whatever reasons, we lost touch. And He gradually became like some playmate waving good-bye from the back of his family's car on the day they moved away, though I can't remember what day that happened.

I wonder now what ever made me stop playing with Him in the first place.

Graduation Night—May, 1973
It's the five of us, standing together on a grassy knoll, dressed in our black caps and gowns, arms linked, proudly posing for the camera, young and bold and ready to embark on unknown adventures. The band is breaking up, heading off to different cities, different schools, different futures. Far in the background, beyond the high school, the sun has fallen into the woods, leaving the sky

brushed with gentle hues of violet and vermilion,
our fine spring day all but done...

My childhood, elusive and beautiful—head up, poised,
listening—had dashed away like a deer through the
woods, a vivid dream barely glimpsed and then gone, van-
ishing with my waking. The time had come to leave. Far
too immature to have formed any sort of plan, my bags
were packed more with feelings than thought, driven by a
firm dissatisfaction, and an unfocused yet ambitious
anger. Unable to identify its source, I directed this resentment at my family, my friends, myself. I even felt angry
with my little town, the place that had so blessed me
growing up. I couldn't wait to leave. There had to be
more out there: more adventure, more excitement, more
women and music and *life* waiting to be consumed.

So long and good riddance—I thought then, not realizing what was really causing me to run away—*So long*
little town and all you little people with your little
dreams. So long little high school and all your suffocating
classrooms and dreary hallways and worn-out textbooks
full of worthless nonsense. So long to all of you in this
dusty old place with your dusty ideas and drab day-in
day-out lives. There's nothing for me here any more.

Party Time.

⧚⧚

We're parked in front of the dorm. It has been a somewhat silent trip, not cold, though not very cozy, either. We
get out, and Dad helps me lift my bags out of the trunk.

Momma sits in the car, staring straight ahead through the windshield, her jaw slightly slack.

"Well, son," Dad is saying, as if the time has come when he is expected to say something, "This can be the start of the next phase of your life," or something like that. "Yes, sir," I mumble. I don't know what else to say, and neither does he. I have become more and more quiet my last few years at home. I have not learned how to tell my parents I will miss them, or to even thank them. So my father and I shake hands, and I walk around to Mom's window and lean in, kissing her cheek.

"Good-bye, Mom," I say. And her face is caught somewhere between frustration and medication and fear and love and great sorrow, her eyes wet.

"Goodbye, honey," she says. "You be a good boy."

And so began my hopeless quest—trying to fill some deep, inner emptiness with every worldly thing I could find. I chose college in Memphis without a single academic consideration. It met my only real criteria: a large city with a good party reputation, two hundred miles from where I lived, which seemed at the time both close enough and far enough away. Looking back, I can see clearly now how completely unprepared I was to leave home and go into the world.

I had little interest in being a student. I majored in journalism, but dropped out as soon as I discovered the professors had no intention of teaching me how to become the next Great American Novelist. I signed up for as many philosophy courses as allowed, trying to avoid as much math as possible. For a while I enjoyed these classes, with their brainy give-and-take discussions, the stretching of thoughts, the searching for "meaning," whatever that meant. We studied the usual spread of philosophers, some well known like Socrates and Plato, and others more obscure (at least to me). I tried to cultivate a connection with these pursuers of knowledge. Most of what they wrote—particularly anything to do with topics that were to me as incomprehensible as mathematics and physics—I simply skipped over. But I grew proficient at searching out anything in their writings that I thought might validate my own selfishness, bending their truths to my own, and thereby becoming a sort of philosophical revisionist-of-convenience. "If you would be a real seeker of truth," wrote Descartes, "you must at least once in your life doubt, as far as possible, all things." And this sounded about right to me at the time, appropriately taken out of context, since I had learned by then to doubt virtually everything, and to trust no one. I roughly translated *Cogito Ergo Sum* as, "I drink, therefore I need not think." But after a while it all became mostly tiresome, and my impression was that the majority of students on campus fell into two basic categories: those who believed philosophy to be The Great Essence Of All Truth, and those who considered it The Great Crock Of All Crap. I couldn't quite decide on which side I belonged, and so ultimately chose to belong on neither.

All along I expanded my list of authors, and poets. I adored Whitman and Dickinson, Robert Browning and T. S. Eliot. And Frost was still a favorite. I'd read "The

Road Not Taken" in high school, of course—*Two roads diverged in a wood, and I—I took the one less traveled by / And that has made all the difference*—and it had predictably appealed to my sense of adventure. But now I dug deeper—*I dwell in a lonely house I know / That vanished many a summer ago*—discovering a kinship. *I dwell with a strangely aching heart / In that vanished abode there far apart / On that disused and forgotten road...*

I dove into Dostoevski, Bergson, and Virgil and Dante and Goethe, just to appear superior, and Henry James and D.H. Lawrence, and finally to the likes of Dreiser and Nin and Henry Miller, devouring everything I could lay my hands on, fascinated by the shameless, shocking mixture of the reverent and the blasphemous, the profane and profound, dazzling prose that was vile and vulgar and often unabashedly brilliant. I didn't give a hoot about their politics; but I hungrily sought anything resembling a kindred spirit of self-destruction. I escaped between the covers of these books, and loved them all.

Strangely, I held no interest in studying music. I attended a few music theory classes, found them inexpressibly boring, and never returned. My dream was never one of becoming a great composer or musician. I'd never had much curiosity concerning the "bones" of music, the mathematics of it, though admittedly this might have had more to do with laziness than artistic intention. But for me, really, it was never *about* the music; it was about communicating and sharing, using simple melody as a vehicle for all the thoughts and feelings forever rumbling around in the depths of me, planning their escape. It was about storytelling. I grasped for the language I had never learned to speak, a way to finally connect with all the people whom until that point had looked at me as if I had two heads. Music, then and now, felt almost magical. And I've never cared to know how the trick is performed.

The only college class in which I felt really involved was Creative Writing. Thinking myself uniquely talented, I turned in a short story expecting to amaze the professor. A few days later he handed it back to me, marked simply, "Try Again." Astonished at his lack of perception and appreciation, I approached him after class.

"You write well," he said dryly, peering over his glasses, clearly less than dazzled. "But I suggest you try writing about something you have actually experienced. Something you *know*."

And I did, composing a piece about a girl I had met, a dark story telling of a night in her apartment—an eerie place, haunting and hushed, with incense burning and the lights low…describing how, later, with the gray moonlight coming through the bedroom window onto her pale and empty face, she half-spoke, half-whispered that she was dying of cancer.

My paper came back marked with an A+, and the words "That's It."

Mostly, though, school functioned as a place to hide. Here I began to drink and drug with regularity. I was a late starter; I had never really considered drinking to get drunk while in high school, instead developing other methods of medication. I had stayed busy—busy dreaming, obsessed with trying to find some false sense of intimacy and trust with the girls I dated, busy trying to belong to someone, to something. But eighteen was the legal drinking age in 1974, and from the first time my buddies and I left our dorm rooms and headed for the city bars, I recognized a difference in the *way* I drank. Something told me early on that I was going to be good at it.

One night, I had a revelation. In some ways, this would be one of the most important events of my life. I believed I had found my purpose, and what I thought to be my destiny, at a nondescript bar called Silky's.

We all sat there around the table, flushed with new-found freedom, feeling very mature and very young, frightened and fearless there in the city. We ordered a tray full of something—whiskey sours I believe, not having any idea what a whiskey sour was—and we toasted our limitless new lives, and drank. I liked it. A lot. I remember an instantaneous, immense feeling of *relief*—sweet relief, that this sensation I had been secretly seeking for most of my young life could somehow be attained through the simple act of swallowing. I knew I had found my missing piece. It was as though I had discovered the magic elixir, the stuff that filled the mysterious emptiness within. It flowed through me, warm and healing, like the syrup that had rushed through my veins in the old gymnasium, only this time the affect was relatively effortless, and immediate. The chatter in my head, that noise always hammering away at me, began to dull and quiet, to turn from a roar into a hum, and I began to feel safe and strong and confident. Within minutes I felt less afraid, less *alone.* For the very first time in my life, I seemed to completely understand everything everyone else was saying. And, astonishingly, they seemed to better understand me, too, as if a switch had been turned on, something like the Universal Translator on Star Trek— suddenly we were all speaking the same language. That feeling of not quite fitting in with the world around me began to disappear, and I felt wise and powerful. *This is it*—I thought, my heart leaping inside me—*this is what I have been seeking. Everything makes perfect sense now.*

We ordered more. Though the others stopped after a few, I stayed at it. I could not understand, even on that first night, why anyone would voluntarily stop drinking. The bar was still open. We still had money. The night was still young. And with each drink, my thirst increased.

Standing at the urinal in the bathroom, I decided as an experiment to let my head fall forward into the concrete wall. I heard a thud, coming from far away. And just as I had hoped, I didn't feel a thing.

From that point on, I did a lot of drugs. But always I turned to alcohol as my drug of choice. It medicated me where I hurt the most, becoming my best friend, and ultimately my worst enemy. It took time, of course. Young and healthy, with enough light remaining to keep the drink from consuming me for a while, I considered myself invulnerable. But a process had begun. I had discovered what appeared to be a way out. I had tasted something that I mistook for peace.

Later, I experimented with LSD, riding around in a car with a bunch of friends through the streets of the city, tripping my brains out. At first it was wonderful, joyous and liberating, like the shedding of spiritual skin. Trying to use words to describe an acid trip is at best ludicrous; but at some point, I went insane. I remember starting to cry, right there with all my peers. There in the back seat, worlds apart from everything, I began to feel a familiar, immense loneliness; only this time the sense of separateness took on shape and texture, slashing at me, a razor-sharp wedge being forced between my existence and all other life. *Do you love me?*—Certain no one loved me, and so I cried, out loud, again and again—*Do you really love me? Am I okay? Are you my friends? Please, please...help me...love me...save me...*

The pain of that night, and the time-span involved, seems immeasurable; the rest of the nightmare is lost. But waking in my room the following morning I lay mortified in bed, an enormous dread weighing down on me, saturated with shame and guilt. I looked up and saw my roommate getting dressed.

"Man, you really lost it last night," he said, not bothering to conceal the sarcasm.

"I did?"—Naked and ashamed, exposed, remorseful.

"Yeah," he said, a little impatiently. "You freaked us all out." He put on his shoes and walked to the door. "You kept asking us to love you," he said. He started to say something else, then just slightly shook his head, and left.

My misery would not allow me to leave the room that day. Not long after, I dropped out of college.

≋≋

Soon after leaving school I formed a musical partnership with a friend. His name was Kenny. He lived with his girlfriend in an apartment, and right away I could see how such an arrangement was far superior to being in college.

We hit it off. We loved the same kinds of music—Crosby, Stills, Nash & Young, Pink Floyd, Steely Dan, Yes, The Who, Billy Joel, James Gang, Traffic, Supertramp, and harder stuff, too, like the Allman Brothers and Lynyrd Skynyrd and Led Zeppelin. He played guitar, and though neither of us were very good musicians, there is no evidence that we were ever aware of that fact. In short time we had formed a duo, performing around town at steakhouse bars and Holiday Inn lounges. We had a certain chemistry, and shared the same dream—eventually we added a bass player, then a drummer, then another guitarist, until finally we had become what both of us always wanted: a real live rock-and-roll band.

We lived and rehearsed at an idyllic spot nick-named "The Ranch"—three rented houses outside the city, on land that had once been some sort of boy's camp in the fifties. The rent was dirt cheap, and not a neighbor in sight. For nearly three years we lived in Hippie Paradise Found, playing as loud and getting as high as we wanted. Lots of partying. Lots of girls. A time of freedom and discovery for all of us, a time before we knew what life in the "real" world really was—and perhaps a time when we knew more about living than we even realized.

We spent these three years in Memphis playing local clubs, developing our style and sound. This was a rich time, and I felt more whole, pledging myself to this new family, all of us joined together by our hopes, trusting and depending on one another to accomplish the improbable. Loading our gear into our beat-up cars, we roared into town like gunslingers, playing every saloon that had a stage, and some that didn't. Chugging down our beers and cranking up our amps, we flew unencumbered by musical rules or knowledge through an era of unfettered, exhilarating expression. People loved us.

I wrote most of the songs, free verse visions of innocent love and young hopes and daring dreams. It's often easy to look back on the silliness of our pasts and overlook the fact that much of what we were then was better in some ways than what we have been since. Because even though we were reckless and selfish and had no real focus at the time, we still lived very much like children, full of energy and talent that knew no boundaries, a spine-tingling, breathless joy splashing out of us whether we recognized it or not. None of us had musical training. None of us had a clue, unwilling to accept the laws of physics that said we couldn't fly. We flourished there in those smoky neon bars, late night into early morning, life turned up loud, hearts beating to the powerful pulse of distant drums, surging, soaring, fearless.

Three years later, we did what seemed absolutely logical. We decided to move the entire five-piece band to Los Angeles, where the record companies and TV and the movies and even more girls were, waiting. I felt certain the gods of Stardom had been maintaining constant vigilance in expectation of our triumphant arrival, and I somehow had been able to convince the rest of the band that it would be unconscionable for us to disappoint them. We had little money, no contacts, and virtually no idea what we were doing or how we would do it once we got there. We made, in the purest sense, a leap of faith. Dangerous. Reckless. *Perfect.*

The bass player and I began the two thousand mile journey in my 1968 Volkswagen Bug, armed with less than two hundred dollars, and two trash bags stuffed full of clothes. The car had no working heater, and had once been wrecked so badly that air now poured through every part of the dash. We duct-taped the thing as best we could, and at one point during the trip as we headed over the mountains had to drape blankets across us to keep from freezing.

I still see clearly Memphis at dusk as we drove away, the lights of the city becoming like stars, then dim, then gone. I felt both fearless and afraid, and deeply alive, the way explorers must have always felt. As the night grew dark around us, I experienced an intoxication that ran like sparks up and down and through every part of me. I had absolutely no idea what would happen to me. It was exhilarating. And from somewhere deep in the still-hungry child of me I wanted to scream—TURN LEFT HERE! STRAIGHT THROUGH THAT GATE!—becoming as lost as I possibly could, far and forever into the distant country, down and deep into the hooded woods. And this time, I would succeed.

Amazingly, the car made it. I think God was still with me.

Part Three

running away

And not many days later,
the younger son
gathered everything together
and went on a journey
into a distant country,
and there he squandered
his estate with loose living.
—*Luke 15:13*

————————

So I'll tell you
what I have decided to do...
I'm off to the city
of Solla Sollew
On the banks of the
beautiful River Wah-Hoo,
Where they never have troubles!
At least, very few.
—*Dr. Seuss*

the distant country

I'm standing on the HOLLYWOOD *sign.* Something made me want to climb up there from the moment I laid eyes on it, this thing of legend leaning out from the side of the canyon. We hadn't been in town long, maybe a few weeks. But already we had found new friends and followers, willing to show us around, to help us find the best dope, to join in and become part of the fame they saw us destined for. And when on one particularly fine evening, after getting high all day and going from one famous place to another, one of them said to me—What do you want to do tonight? I didn't hesitate—The Sign!

Remembering. There are six or seven of us. We had waited until after dark, so the cops wouldn't chase us away. Now that we're finally up the steep hill of scrub and rock, it appears less awe-inspiring than expected; after years of neglect and weather and occasional vandalism, the thing looks anything but famous. This monument to movies and magic and money which had appeared so huge and white and permanent from the city streets below now hung unceremoniously on its hill, nothing more than wood and steel and bolts and screws, rotting and rusting, with large missing pieces and bird droppings and flaking paint. Still, I'd come this far. Somehow the others manage to boost me up and over, until finally I'm standing right on the crossbar of the H, *the newly crowned king, observing the expanse of his territory. I take a defiant hit on my joint, and blow the smoke straight up in the air, laughing, while the others cheer and applaud. The cool desert night washes over me like healing water, the lights in the valley below sprawled and glittering as if some neon galaxy has crashed to earth.*

This place is mine—I whisper to myself—All mine. And nothing is going to stop me now.

I go to parties, sometimes until four
It's hard to leave when you can't find the door.
—JOE WALSH

We're climbing through Artemus Hammon's window. We'd tried ringing the doorbell and knocking for nearly half an hour. We knew someone rattled around in there; there were no lights on, but we could hear voices yelling and feet running and all sorts of bizarre sounds coming from inside. In the incandescent, never-quite darkness of the L.A. night, the old house looked like some miniature gothic castle silhouetted against the glowing sky.

We had been invited to dinner. In less than two years on the Hollywood club scene, our group had suddenly found itself among the most popular of all the local bands. Artemus Hammon was a record company executive, a real big shot. He liked to hang out at the local nightclubs, searching for talent (and God knows what else). And ever since we had become one of the top weekend club draws, Hammon had been keeping an eye on us.

Our success had been both unlikely and meteoric, though in my mind at least all within perfect reason. My dreams were coming true, rapidly. And now Hammon had *personally* asked Kenny and me over to discuss "possibilities." Hammon was connected to everybody in the L.A. music business. We considered ourselves balanced on the edge of greatness.

For the moment, though, we were knocking, and the door of opportunity would not open. We stood at the arched entrance and banged again with a brass knocker shaped like a goat's head. We pressed our ears to the door and heard shouts, bellowed commands followed by child-like yelps and squeals of fear. Looking at each other, we smiled. It hadn't taken us long; we had come to grips with the fact that the entire desert wonderland was blissfully, completely mad, and in fact had come to embrace it.

Finally we heard the sound of feet approaching, and the lock being thrown. The door opened a crack, then stopped hard, something large and heavy blocking the way. "Push!" yelled a childlike voice, and push we did, but the door wouldn't budge more than a few inches. Again, the sound of bare feet slapping against hardwood, running away. Then, "TELL THEM TO CRAWL THROUGH THE DAMNED WINDOW!" A thunderous voice, that of Zeus, coming from somewhere far within the house, yet still shaking the windows. Then the little feet again, and an almost-whisper through the crack: "He wants you to come through the window."

It must have looked like a scene from a Laurel and Hardy movie, the two of us trying to crawl up the brick wall of that mansion, Kenny holding the window as I fell through onto a pile of half-packed cardboard boxes. He followed, and we sat on the floor looking around us through dim shadows at what appeared to be the aftermath of an explosion—boxes, clothes, furniture strewn everywhere, a beautiful dining table turned on its side, blocking the front door. The immense room was a shambles. Staring at us with total disregard stood a young boy, no more than fourteen or fifteen years old, dressed only in bikini underwear.

"Artie is waiting for you in the bedroom," he said.

We were escorted down a long hall and into a room nearly filled with an immense canopy bed. Candles in ornate silver holders provided the only light, and we again found ourselves surrounded by indistinguishable mountains of more chaos, making it almost impossible to walk through the mess. Incense and dope smoke hung like a heavy blue cloud halfway between our heads and the twelve-foot ceiling. Several young boys stood around the room, barely dressed. Outrageous artwork leaned from the walls, some beautiful and some macabre, and above the bed hung an absurdly ornate framed mirror the size of a pool table. As if in some imagined scene from a Roman orgy, we had been ushered into the great throne room of Caligula—all madness and excess, half a dozen boys clad in various kinds of underwear and silk bathrobes, flittering in and out of the room like butterflies, their squeals occasionally punctuated by a booming voice shouting obscenities. And there, sitting on the edge of the bed, sat the Great Hammon.

He might have been as old as sixty back then, though he had the kind of face that made it hard to tell his age. Artemus Hammon sat on his bed-throne with a sort of dignified decadence, a repulsive yet redoubtable figure, simultaneously emanating nobility and wretchedness. A dangerous fool, part Shakespeare and part Dickens, he held his unshaven chin high as Othello, dramatically perched on the bony pick-pocket fingertips of Fagin, as if posing for a painter's portrait. His long, stringy gray hair hung halfway down his back, the jagged nose cutting through his face like a dagger, eyes set deep and close together. He projected a formidable presence, even in this hysterical setting, wearing a silk kimono painted with warring dragons, flames streaking from their mouths. He seemed mad enough to yell "Off with their heads!" and commanding enough to have it done.

We entered the room to violent screams: "DAMN YOU! GET ME MY SLIPPERS BEFORE I FEED YOU ALL TO THE DOGS!" One arm made a slow, graceful flourish, as if gathering a handful of lightning bolts. The boys scattered like mice. Hammon turned to us, great silver eyebrows lifting like falcons taking flight, noticing our presence for the first time.

We stood very still. He smiled, slowly, running the pointed tip of his tongue over a thin bottom lip. Holding out his right hand, palm up, the Emperor closed his thumb and first three fingers one at a time into a fist, leaving his little finger extended. The nail was at least an inch long, painted red, and filled with white powder.

"Well?" he leered, aiming his steel-gray right eye over the hook of his nose. "Aperitif?"

It's strange looking back on the years in Los Angeles. I spent nearly a decade of my life there, and yet the truly clear memories all pressed together might only comprise a year, or two. They come floating in like fantasy, dreamparts of me not completely connected to the who and what of me today, some of it real, some not.

I could easily paint this picture in black and white, portraying L.A. as the bad guy, a Sodom and Gomorrah of darkness and sin, as if my going there caused the fall. But the portrait would not be entirely accurate. Los Angeles County has about ten million people living, working, raising families, worshipping, going to school. It is a vast

place, and most of it is something other than moral waste-
land. But there are areas within its borders that exist as a
separate kind of reality, a sort of island culture not quite
connected to the rest of the country. And in that place,
like all places, there lives both Good and Evil. Let's just
say that in certain parts of L.A. the approach to sin can be
somewhat shameless. Babylon with smog.

Which of course made the place everything I'd been
seeking all along: Perfection. Like those backwoods trips
with Mamaw, there was something exhilarating about the
place, a sort of lost-ness with a purpose. Driving into the
city on that very first night, seeing the city lights spread
out before me like an immense spider's web, the night air
sparkling on the strands in a million pulsing colors, I
somehow knew that all bets were off. There was inside
my chest a heart both pounding and fearless.

The first few weeks in town, we had focused our
efforts on finding a place to live. It took us a while to find
something suited to our needs; none of us had ever encoun-
tered such a crowded place, with people living so close
together. But eventually the five of us combined our money
and rented a wretched little hole in Hollywood, a three-
room desolation in the back part of a building that housed
the Black Cat Theatre, a XXX joint located on one of the
less-savory blocks of Santa Monica Boulevard. In this seedy
section of the city we were able to crank up our amps and
rehearse without interference from the neighbors; apparently there was so much drug dealing and prostitution and
God-knows-what-else going on around us that few who
lived in our neighborhood ever dared call the cops.

At first, we all got jobs. I painted houses for a while. Later, I would rise before dawn and drive a courier truck up into the high desert to deliver bank bags to Edwards Air Force Base. Some days, if I were running on schedule, I would park just outside a gate and watch the fighter jets twist and turn in the just-glowing sky. Returning to the city, I'd fight through the San Fernando Valley traffic with my own death-defying maneuvers, listening to rock'n'roll radio. *That'll be me someday*—I thought.

And, of course, there was the ocean—which, oddly enough, felt like a long lost friend. A few times, when I was a kid, our family had vacationed in Panama City Beach, Florida. And I had loved the ocean from the first moment I saw it. We didn't go very often, maybe three or four times. But even then I'd felt an immediate kinship with the sea, one never forgotten. I loved the smell of it, and the vastness, and the sense it gave of my being very small and very meaningless in the big picture of life, and therefore somehow less responsible. I would sit for the longest time and watch the tireless pulse of the earth against the shore, and stare out at the endless horizon and dream of other worlds out there, other mysteries, realities different than my own. I couldn't have put it into words back then. But I knew. I knew He was there—out there in that unfathomable expanse, in that unseen, fog-covered and forever-old place, His Hand having formed it in the very beginning—and that by kneeling at its edge I could somehow draw nearer to Him. The sea made me feel peaceful and yet strangely sad, as though the young boy in me was being drawn to a place from which he had been separated for a very long time, attracted by a familiar voice on the salty wind he couldn't quite make out.

And now, finally reconciled, sitting on the sand of another coast, surrounded by the sounds of kids playing and gulls crying and waves crashing, I almost felt as though I had been born from this deep and mysterious place, had returned as if by destiny, and would one day die there—that until this time there had been some part of me always longing for the sea, this place that wasn't really home, yet somehow held hidden meaning. Reunited, the strange call finally answered, I could stand now at the shore and look out into the mist for hours, any time I wanted, my only real quiet, hidden from the mad rush of my ambition. I spent as much time there as possible, the sun streaking my hair and baking my skin. The other guys thought it was a cool place to visit. For me, it always felt like heaven.

Stage—The Whiskey—1979
*Someone took the photograph from the balcony of the club, at the end of a performance. I'd sent it home to the family, and somehow it had made it into the box. The five of us, arms around each other's shoulders, like brothers, the lights showering down red and gold. Behind us hangs a huge banner, hand-painted by one of our fans, that reads in florid white script—*STAGE...

During these early years in California I began to embrace a philosophy of living that was at once both liberating and life-threatening. I suppose the script is not uncommon: Boy or girl leaves small town in search of fame and fortune, falls to the temptations of Big City Sin and becomes morally corrupt. I dove whole-heartedly into the lifestyle. I worshipped decadence as my god—with a vengeance.

We inhabited another lifetime. There were long days of beach and sun, and climbing up the canyon hills above the city to stare in wonder at the endless sea of colors spread out below, the glorious days sweeping overhead on the sails of white clouds, washing us in alternating waves of shadow and light. We were young, and invulnerable, and filled with purpose.

At night, we wowed the audiences in The Troubadour and The Whiskey and other clubs, and all along I'm having the time of my life, or so I thought—the screaming fans, the all-night parties complete with admirers and record company execs and druggies straight out of Central Casting, the sordid dressing rooms filled with willing groupies, the shameless and reckless orgies of over-indulgence, chugging champagne and snorting rails of cocaine from the tops of toilets.

We had beaten the odds. We called the band "Stage," as in Shakespeare's *who struts and frets his hour upon*, a clumsy attempt on my part to imbue the group with a sort of literary significance that no doubt went unnoticed by most fans. Still, something was working. *"Their offbeat, jazz-inspired rock holds the makings for a fine album,"* wrote one reviewer in none other than *The Los Angeles Times*. We may have had no idea what we were doing, but we must have been doing it right. We were *making it!* The mad, swirling lunacy of it all seemed unstoppable. *I* was unstoppable, taking to the stage as if I had been born there, writing songs that seemed to come magically from a place far beyond myself, as if some force of pure spirit was propelling me at the speed of light, performing without a net, without experience or planning or regard for reality, raising my fists in the air, hair halfway down my back, a *Star*, by God, flying there under the colored lights like a pro, born for it, and nothing was going to get in my way.

This is what I was made for, I thought. *This is what I am...*

"*Well, gentlemen,*" *he is saying, his face gaunt and shadowed, lifting another nail-full of coke to his enormous nostril. Snort, sniff, eyes roll back, then re-focus on us. "*How does it feel to be, shall we say...on the verge?*" *Then, as a couple of boys are caught edging their way toward us and closer to the drugs, our host rises to his full imposing height, spreading out his arms like Moses about to declare the law, towering over us and everything else in his universe—*"*BE GONE, YOU WORTHLESS WORMS! I'LL SKIN THE WHOLE LOT OF YOU, SO HELP ME GOD!*" *And when they run, Hammon turns, his snarl suddenly a smile. He looks almost wistfully down on us, a demented kindness softening his face, just for a moment.*

"*I love these boys,*" *he says softly.*

And in that strange little apartment full of drums and amps, rehearsing day after day, eating pizza and drinking beer out there on that distant planet a million miles from earth, we took each day as if it belonged to us and no one else, the ones willing to risk and to dare. For a short while, it seemed the world would soon be ours.

We had developed a rabid following. There were plenty of young people looking for something or someone with whom they could join forces, and to whom they could swear loyalties. As the lead singer of this new, fresh-faced group of boys with funny southern accents, I found myself the focus of much-desired adoration, now center stage. All of this attention made perfect sense to me. I had been expecting it all my life, in a way, and also dreading deep down any possibility of it never happening. So long starving for something, I had now arrived at the world's biggest smorgasbord. I began to gorge. Each time I played to a wild, cheering crowd, I could feel myself becoming more powerful, more sure of my invincibility. And I became convinced that the world and everything in it was mine to use.

Over time, my addictions grew. As much as with alcohol and drugs, another need began to possess me. I spent enormous time and energy with my "little black book." At first this behavior seemed perfectly natural; after all, who could resist all these women now available to me? But in time I became as obsessed with this compulsion as with chemicals. I did not want to spend the night alone; the very thought of it frightened me, though I couldn't have recognized it as fear at the time. Terrified of commitment, I was even more afraid of being by myself. And like any drug, this need was progressive, ever escalating, always driving me towards more and more, night after night shamelessly preying, using, discarding, and using again. Looking back now, I can barely recognize the person I was then—treating people like animals, with no regard for them or myself, roaming the city nights with the morals of an alley cat.

I embraced far too much lust in my life to allow for love. But there was one girl. Somehow she managed to get further in, at least for a while. Perhaps we really were in love, to the degree I could allow and comprehend such a thing. In the midst of the madness only she was able to capture at least a part of my heart, the part still barely beating, and perhaps in some way to influence my survival, though she would never know it.

Her name was Emilia. A successful actress, she made enough money to buy her widowed mother a house in the San Gabriel Valley. She spoke three languages fluently. She had the soul of a poet, and a passion for art.

Emilia came by her gifts honestly. Her mother, Maria, was a wonderful eccentric, poet, former cabaret singer, once long-ago married to the President of Venezuela; a framed photograph on her mantel pictured him sitting aristocratically atop a beautiful black horse, wearing a sombrero the size of a pup tent. From her large leather chair the fine lady, dressed for our visit in old, lacy black dresses, would tell stories of the time long ago when she sang sad songs in the cafes of Europe. As she spoke, her eyes sparkled like those of a young girl. And in this museum living room stuffed with decades of memories and antiques, Emilia's mother would sometimes sit at the ancient, hand-carved piano, and in a voice like a valuable old vase—cracked but not yet emptied of passion—sing to us melodies and words from a time more romantic, when love meant forever.

Emilia understood me in ways I did not yet understand myself. Both of us knew, I think, that what we shared was powerful, something that would in fact have changed us both even more had I ever found the courage to allow it. I fought it, because I realized she would require more of me than I had to give. And for a while she was able to spend long and intense stretches of days and nights with me, then let me go, never quite sure if or when I might return. She often offered but never insisted that I stay, and though I would sometimes leave a shirt or pair of shoes in her closet, I could never bring myself to move in, to surrender to her my wildness or my fear.

Still, again and again, I came back. Together we walked the humming streets of Hollywood, reverently stepping around the Stars embedded in the famous sidewalk. We ate the strange and wonderful ethnic foods I'd grown to love, and watched old movies at the Rialto or the Fox Venice, arms locked, mesmerized by old black and white prints of Chaplin or Bette Davis movies or cult foreign films, tirelessly sitting through double features eating popcorn after midnight.

Occasionally we took trips to San Francisco, walking those streets for hours, entranced by the heady romance of the place. With the sun going down orange and scarlet into the bay, I could almost pretend I was someone else, someone in a movie, maybe, with different possibilities, a different heart. But by the time we returned to Los Angeles not much about my heart had really changed at all. The nights transformed me, and my old roles returned. I would leave her apartment in the gray early morning, running away, back out to my music, other lovers, other addictions. And she never said much, always there, waiting, when I came back. She knew what I was, and was drawn to it, and afraid of it, and in time would both love and hate me.

She warned me, later, of what I was becoming. She was one of the first to see the darkness on its way, and wisely turn from it.

Thinking that the light in me was my own, slowly but predictably I began to dim. The change didn't happen overnight, and many around me weren't fully aware at first. But I was being drawn, irresistibly, towards a lost place. And now my reading list began to change, too. I trudged through the grim existentialist novels, finding a kind of sordid solace alongside these artisans of suffering. I explored Camus and Nietzsche and Sartre, all seemingly entranced by the darkness they painted, embracing the night as if they belonged there. They seemed to both defy and deify pain. Their tortured characters became my new heroes.

I could never get enough. Never. The more I drank and smoked and snorted, the more women I slept with, the more debauched my daily living, the less satisfied I became. And it was then that even those racing alongside began to fall away. Once the tone of things moved from recreational to deadly serious, many left the party, and only the truly hardcore users hung around. As far as I was concerned, if you couldn't party at my speed and intensity, I had little use for you. I was a professional.

The things we remember, and the things we forget. The better part of ten years, now a scattered, surreal collection of sensations, part memory, part dream-come-true, part nightmare, the biggest part of who I am, and no part at all. The reality of it lodges in memory as time disjointed, jarred and broken and no longer linear, just a smear of thought that still startles me, almost a decade of my life floating past my mind, a storm cloud nothing less than cataclysmic, yet nothing more than a curl of smoke.

And as I look back into that time and place, I see lights...colored lights, and night that was never quite dark, and people everywhere, searching for something. I hear loud music, and the sound of people laughing too loud and the clinking of glasses, the wailing of souls...I smell exhaust and rubber and sun-baked pavement, endless miles of pavement, and dope smoke and perfume and sweat and, somewhere, faintly, the salt of the sea. I remember the streets that wound in and around themselves like endless, headless serpents, and the incongruous palm trees straining pitifully from their ocean of concrete, there in that gorgeous, filthy, shimmering, red-haze of endless summer. I can still see the beauty of the long, bright-blue days, the perfect people, the Mercedes Benz-lined boulevards and the Beverly Hills chic, a sort of plastic perfection that was almost stunningly attractive, yet somehow untouchable, like a holographic image real enough to reach for, but not to feel...the days full of color and light and, on some level, *dreams,* the real fuel of the place, a dream-driven energy driving many of the inhabitants blissfully insane. It doesn't look all that dangerous to me now, this memory of the days.

But the nights. I remember the nights differently. It's here that the dream becomes more sense than thought, more sensation than visual. I remember the nights as something altogether separate and alive, and still even now I can close my eyes and smell it, take a deep breath and taste it, roll it around on my tongue like familiar, irresistible poison...the sheer excess of it all, the gluttony of desire, a sort of feeding-frenzy that once started wouldn't stop until our teeth hit bone. I remember the thick, drugged air and the sweet-stale buzz of humanity, crushed together like insects, feeding off each other, stealing each other's breath and blood and want...cigarettes and whiskey, the bars and nightclubs with their mirrors and back-lit bottles that became like close, trusted, deceitful friends...the taste of lipstick and the hollow fury of sex without love, the animal clinging and scratching and hoping against hope that we might find something deeper than ourselves if we could just steal enough from the bodies we held, taking and taking and destroying and being destroyed, all of us locked together in some futile dance of need, desperately linked like a train headed for a gap in the tracks, thrill-ride turned slowly but surely into something less than thrilling, but now going way too fast to jump off...

Looking back through some heady fog, at a place that wasn't real and a time that wasn't real and yet both so fully a part of me that I'll never quite wake from it, from this dream that isn't a dream at all, this place of plastic mist and tears and neon and chrome, children masquerading as rock stars and actors and whores and saviors, the angels and the devils, the lame and the blind and the leper all lined up outside the bars at midnight, pockets full of cash, waiting to join the dance...tearing through each others lives, cruel and reckless, slaves to desire, lost together in this hollow land filled with the fantasy of false gods...life exhilarating and horrible, life lived to the fullest and to the most shallow, a seemingly Godless time in which He had probably never before or since wrapped Himself so tightly around me. And looking back now, though much of it all seems so unreal, I know one truth that runs deep in my flesh: Every time I turned my back on Him, He was always facing me.

❧

We're about to climb back out into the coming morning, the so-called business meeting deteriorating into decadence we want no part of. The madness was fascinating for a while, but we decide to make our escape before having to witness any greater atrocities. And Hammon is leaning over us, clearly disappointed, the emperor and his intended victims, peering over that great hawk-beak of a nose. "It is not true that you must sell your soul to the devil," he said, his voice softening to a near whisper. "If you get close enough," he said, eyes flickering like candles, "you'll give it to him for free." He uncurled his little finger like a talon. "Contrary to popular belief," he hissed, "the devil doesn't make any bargains, boys..."

Mamaw would send me letters.

"It sure seems boring around this little town without you here," she wrote. "Everyone misses you. But we all know you are going to accomplish wonderful things. Everybody says to tell you hello. Papaw says keep your nose clean. And always know that we are here for you, that we love you, and that you can always come home. Love, Mamaw"

Kenny and I took long drives, cruising up the winding roads above the city, high on weed and our heady ambition. As the sun set, we'd sit on a grassy ledge, watching the cars quietly climbing like colored ants up and down their canyon trails, and talk about things to come, greatness and wealth and fame, and sometimes even of deeper things. And if he saw me changing, he never said much, maybe because he wasn't quite ready for the ride to end just yet.

One night, after sitting still and quiet for a few moments above the hum of the red and yellow and purple city, my friend startled me. His words seemed unrelated to our reality, at least the reality I could see. We felt close to signing our record deal. But success had brought with it a kind of gradual erosion, one paralleling my own slow demise, one I of course fully denied. He had been somewhat distant, and thoughtful. Still, I didn't expect his question.

"In all of this," he said, looking out at the night, "in all of what's going on, do you ever have thoughts about…"—he hesitated—"about God?"

I had been lying on my back in the grass, and I sat up immediately, as if shaken awake. We had always been able to talk, to share our feelings. But this caught me by surprise. I didn't want to talk about this.

"Oh yeah, sure," I said, trying to sound nonchalant, my mind suddenly darting, looking for cover. Something in his question alarmed and threatened. "I've been through all that stuff," I said defensively. "Religion interested me for…for a while," suddenly stammering, "but not anymore…"—*Why am I acting like this? Why do I feel so afraid?* Then—"Hey, I know a lot about religion," I lied, badly, then something like— "and believe me, it's all crap, all of it." I was over-reacting; Kenny saw it instantly, knowing me, and tensed. I didn't let up, kept on about the sham of it all, the uselessness of believing in anything other than ourselves, spewing out my barrage of narcissistic nonsense with such pathetic forced bravado that the air between us turned suddenly dense. Out of the corner of my eye I saw the growing disgust on his face, and launched harder into my speech, rambling on about

God-knows-what, feeling like a fool yet determined to put out this fire and move on to something else. And though I don't recall how our talk ended, I do remember the drive back into the valley, and how quiet Kenny was, as if he wanted to call me a liar and a self-centered idiot. But he never did.

That night as I lay alone in bed, I couldn't help but think about how strange Kenny's question had made me feel. I had recoiled from his words as if from a flame. I was right about God, of course. But still, I felt uneasy, and determined not to talk about it again.

And so the first five or six years rushed past like a comet, brilliant and dazzling, but leaving behind a trail of cold debris. My life was like an empty cup. And not fully realizing what might be missing, I tried to fill the hole with the most God-less of things.

Gradually, the music faded. Though we had become a more polished performing act, the spark was missing. What had once been wings of creative innocence now folded, descending into nothing more than well-rehearsed self-indulgence. The fans drifted away, grabbing on to newer, shinier shooting stars.

The band had been my family, really. I would have been far too cowardly to attempt the whole L.A. thing without them. We loved each other. And yet as time went on, I grew farther from them and deeper into myself, so that even their friendship became worthless to me. *They're not good enough, anyway—I* thought—*they're only holding me back. They're the reason I'm not famous yet.* My desire to be rid of them, of anyone who really cared about me, began to grow stronger than my desperation to cling to them for protection, for affection. It was all a part of my self-destructive nature gone wild, taking control, so that eventually all I could do was run toward the things that hurt me, and away from the things worth having.

Over time, I could feel myself becoming another creature, changing into something alien and awful. The transformation occurred too slowly for many to notice, too cunning to be found out. Finally the disease dug in so deeply I could no longer remember what I looked like before. My spirit curled into a corner, dying by degrees within the flesh and bone, so that the man I am now can no longer imagine that thing I was then.

Back home, they must have thought I'd gone crazy, which of course I had. One Christmas, after writing a mostly incoherent letter explaining why I would once again be unable to fly back for the holidays, I had a brilliant idea. After selling enough cocaine to amass a credible amount of cash, I went shopping. I bought lots of things. Strange things, most of which I can't remember: clothes and perfume, expensive watches and jewelry, items I thought sure to impress, things that would make them gasp and shake their heads in wonder at my celebrity status. I bought bracelets and necklaces, socks and ties, a cashmere sweater for Mamaw (*surely the finest thing she had ever owned*—I thought), and a huge bottle of White Shoulders for Mom. I stayed up all one night, snorting coke and drinking bourbon and carrying on an excited conversation with myself, loading a huge cardboard box full of the stuff. The next day I squeezed the massive thing into my car and took it to the post office. I felt certain they would be very impressed with me, and would finally see me as a success.

Later, I heard from my sister that the entire family had gathered around the box on Christmas morning, somewhat at a loss. When they finally opened it, there was some oohing and ahhing, I guess, though all of it guarded, and confused. I was crushed to learn that everyone seemed more worried and sad than anything else.

I would hear other things from home. Knowing that my parents would eventually divorce, it came as no shock when I learned that my father had moved out of the house. I blamed him, of course, as I blamed myself, an irrational and futile kind of blame, angry that he had abandoned her, just as I had done, though in some ways I could not imagine him staying. Unwilling to admit the degree of hatred I felt towards myself, I directed the rage at him, at my hometown, at God if there was one, at the unresponsive world around me. Rarely would I allow myself to think of them, my mother and my father and my sisters (both of whom had married and started families of their own), there in that little town, only minutes from one another, yet worlds apart. And though I tried desperately not to know, I learned the terrible truth of my mother, living alone in our old house, hiding away in her bedroom for days at a time with a mason jar of vodka under the bed...delirious, never even going to the bathroom, until friends would come to try and save her, picking her up like a filthy abandoned baby and loading her into the car. I would hear these things. And I would do nothing.

In the ten years I lived in L.A., I went home to visit only a few times. Amazingly, I always seemed able to straighten up my act for these brief trips; laughing, bragging, trying again to be the life of the party, playing for family and friends what had by then become my most difficult role— life-loving, free-spirited, wildly successful, blissfully indulgent rogue. This facade was difficult to maintain. I spent as little time as possible with my family, always running away to Nashville or Memphis, where I might at least more comfortably be whoever I was pretending to be while drunk.

My shame was overwhelming.

❧❧

"I was reading my Bible this morning," the letter started. Her writing was beginning to look unsteady, as if her hand were shaking as she wrote. "I thought of you, and wanted to send the verse along. I don't mean anything by it, other than I want you to know how much I care about you, and how much I—all of us—want to see you happy:

'When I was a child, I used to speak as a child, think as a child, reason as a child; when I became a man, I did away with childish things. For now we see in a mirror dimly, but then face to face; now I know in part, but then I shall know fully just as I also have been fully known. But now abide faith, hope, love, these three; but the greatest of these is love.'

Know that I am always praying for you. Papaw says keep your nose clean. We miss you, my sweet Jimmy. Love, Mamaw"

◈◈

My dreams of a career were crumbling along with my sense of self-worth. The band had finally fallen apart, driven away by my ego as much as anything, collectively giving up, with no strength left in me to hold it together. Everything was dying. The party had turned to something else, the passion of it becoming a reckless binge, an endless orgy without satisfaction, the celebration now nothing more than medication.

I didn't really see it that way at the time, though. I remained delusional, simultaneously convinced of my superiority and loathsomeness. Traumatic events made little impact on me, removed as I was. The night I caused a multi-car pileup on the Hollywood Freeway, for instance. Spaced out and loopy, driving recklessly in heavy rush-hour traffic, I braked too fast and too late. I don't think my taillights were even working; the car following behind crashed into me at full speed. I was thrown through the windshield (which, on a '68 Bug, thankfully pops out in one piece), and found myself sprawled across what was left of the hood, the rear-mounted engine now sitting in my driver's seat. The impact was great enough to hurl my Volkswagen into the car in front of me, and so on and so on, until about a half-dozen cars were involved. Lying there on the crumpled hood, I could see right through the rear window of the car in front; a lady sat there, frozen, gripping the wheel as if she were still driving. I lay on top of, and was covered by, lots of shattered glass. I rolled off, tried to stand, and fell. We were in the far left-hand lane, and I half-crawled over to the shoulder and leaned back against the concrete barrier. It was fascinating: horns honked, radiators spewed, voices cursed. The rest of the lanes blurred by, unconcerned, hundreds and thousands of cars hurling themselves past our wreckage as if nothing could be more common or less interesting, while our lane sat crumpled together and hissing like a wounded dinosaur, waiting to die and be eaten by all the other monsters screeching past. Surreal as it was, it did not strike me as at all unusual, manifesting itself more as a momentary microcosm of what my life had become than as any sort of real event. Looking at the crushed-accordion remains of my vehicle—from which it did not look even remotely possible that anyone could have emerged alive—I did not in any authentic way feel particularly involved. I smelled the burnt rubber and gasoline and exhaust hanging over me, heard the sirens sounding distant warning. But I felt no pain. There were other people in the crashed cars, but I felt no need to make contact with them. Slowly, I wiggled my toes and flexed my knees, and discovered everything in working order. There was not a scratch on me. Almost casually, I stood and walked to the car now fatally attached to the front of my own. Looking in the driver's window, I saw the frozen lady, hands locked on the wheel, mouth slightly open, still staring straight ahead as if waiting for the light to turn green.

But things were okay, really. No big deal. I didn't need a damn car, and I sure as hell didn't need any friends, who were mostly dropping like flies by now. Some who had been drawn to me began to be repelled, while a few with similar self-destructive inclinations hovered near like vultures, attracted to the eminent decay, waiting to pick clean the bones. Many welcomed me in to the pit. Soon, only the addicts seemed like worthy companions, the ones who shared my self-destructive tendencies, the ones perfectly willing to rampage with me through the lives of everyone foolish enough to draw near.

¿"Me amas?"—Her voice husky, breathless, her lips touching my ear. "Do you love me?"— she whispers again, and I try physically to answer her without words, the eternal lights of the city making the room glow, our skin glistening like wet gold... "¿Me amas? Necesito que tú me digas estes palabras"—now more pleading than passionate, but I can't say it, the one lie I've never mastered, can't give her the words she wants, and my eyes are clenched, heart racing, my face buried in the merciful blackness of her hair...

Kenny was packing his things. The rest of the band had been long gone, but Kenny had always hung with me. Now even he couldn't take it anymore.

"Goodbye," he said, looking at me with...what? Pity? Then, he was gone. And I don't recall trying very hard to make him stay; once he left L.A., I would be able to continue on my downward path unencumbered. There would be no one left who had known me before. I could become what I wanted.

The apartment, once so noisy and full, now sat nearly empty. Once everyone had gone, I was surprised to see how little had been left behind. We shared everything; now I realized that almost nothing had really belonged to me. I rearranged the few remaining pieces of old furniture. Everything else fit easily into my tiny bedroom. I was alone.

The music didn't last much longer. I lamely tried putting together another band, but had no more heart for it. I once sobered up long enough to audition with a group looking for a lead singer. It turned out to be four rich Jewish teenagers from Beverly Hills. We were, to say the least, an odd combination. But for some reason, they thought me a perfect fit. I was able to fool them for a while, but it all came crashing down, so to speak, the day we played a big-budget swimming party at someone's mansion. The absurdly rich crowd found it less than amusing when, while drunkenly strutting across the front of an outdoor stage a la Mick Jagger, I stumbled and fell off onto a table of, appropriately enough, dozens of little glasses full of champagne. This marked my final appearance with the guys, who, though understandably angry, were at least able to convince the owner of the mansion not to have me arrested.

Time passed. Slowly. Still pretending. Tarzan. Ilya Kuryakin. Bullet Bob. Preacher. Rock Star. And now a new role:

Expatriate Writer, Misunderstood Artist, Cynical Drunk. I relished my isolated superiority. Sitting alone in my rat hole, I hammered away at the typewriter, filling page after page with hate and resentment and fear, playing my part to the hilt—joint hanging from my mouth, a bottle of cheap bourbon always within reach, for protection, like a weapon cocked and loaded against the loneliness. God only knows what I wrote; trash, all of it, though thankfully now lost. Bitterness, mostly. Frustration aimed at the world for treating me so unfairly, for not recognizing my undiscovered genius...passing out on the couch, waking before dawn, mercilessly pounding the keys some more, until one night in a rage I threw the wretched machine across the bare room, smashing it, rendering it useless. I hurled it from my bedroom window into the alley below, the two resident junkies scattering like rats, cursing.

The typewriter had been a gift from my father. My high school graduation present.

the singing of angels

Fame had absconded. Most of my loyal followers were now loyally following someone or something else—a new band, a new long-haired idol, perhaps. What had once been a kind of Grand Central Station of Rockdom was now a roach-infested nest littered with half-empty pizza boxes and completely empty beer cans and liquor bottles.

The Armenian landlord had been threatening me for weeks. He was a short, stout little fellow, built like a bowling ball. When angry, his dark face would turn the color of strawberries. Sick of my lies, he had begun hammering furiously on my door early every morning, when he knew I was in the most agony, swearing loudly in his native tongue. I didn't understand a word, but the meaning was clear: I had to get out of there, before the cops threw me out.

I owed him several months' rent, but since I hadn't worked in nearly half a year there was little chance of him ever getting a cent out of me, and I suppose he knew that. And so I did what perhaps he hoped for, slipping away under the cover of night, taking with me things I thought important and leaving the rest behind. I congratulated myself on this brilliant bit of espionage, proud of my decadence and daring. The landlord was probably just thrilled to be rid of me.

Though no longer the main attraction, I still had a few believers. One girl put me up in her large house in the canyon, to help me "get my life back together." She was a business big shot, and a sort of music culture junkie, too, vicariously living out her Rock fantasies through people like me. For a while, she found having me around somewhat exciting, as if she were boarding a Jim Morrison clone. But it didn't take long; with me systematically emptying her refrigerator and purse, the novelty of my presence began to wear predictably thin.

Still, she was generous.

"I have just the thing for you," she said one evening, returning from work. She sat on the edge of my bed and looked down at me. Her eyes said this: *"I have to get him out of here, before I come home one night and find him dead.* "But her mouth said: "A friend of mine owns a restaurant up in Alpine Lake. He wants you to come play piano on the weekends."

I didn't speak. My head felt like someone had crammed butter knives under my eyelids and into my skull.

"We're talking good money, and a rent-free cabin," she said, and through the fog I started hearing something that sounded attractive. "And all you have to do is work up some lounge stuff, and sing while everybody eats."

This sounded both horrific and full of promise. I blinked and sat up.

Hope sprang into her eyes. She still believed in me, I think, sure that I would one day return to my rightful place as Super Star. I didn't have the heart to tell her that I had no desire whatsoever to have another band, or to ever sing another note, for that matter.

"The fresh air would do you good," she said. "Clear your head." I must have still looked hesitant. "I'll even loan you my spare Jeep," she said.

I grabbed my head in both hands, trying to keep my brains from spilling out.

"Does this restaurant have a bar?"

Alpine Lake resort sits on top of the San Bernardino Mountains, seven thousand feet above the valleys of Southern California. Once I reached the mountaintop, I thought I'd found Paradise: a picturesque little town, loosely patterned after a Swiss village, full of tourist shops and places to eat and drink. The sky was azure blue, the air clean and cool, the local girls appeared healthy and, if not exactly lonely, at least somewhat bored. It could not have been more perfect—a cabin all to myself, sing a few songs three nights a week, establish a warm, compassionate friendship with my very own bartender. Yes. This would do. Strolling through the picturesque village square, I felt almost hopeful.

As soon as I found the cabin, I knew that here was a wonderful place to hide. Rustic, but with all the pleasures of home. *A great place to create*—I thought, standing in my new abode, nodding nobly. I opened all the windows and let the crisp mountain air flow through. This was right out of the movies: high above L.A., separated from my defeat, I could play a new role, and start a new false life. I could be the official Village Drunken Artist. It was as if, like a tumor, I had been removed from my sick host and transplanted into a new and unsuspecting body. *No one knows me here*—I thought. I almost felt happy.

I even had my own bird. The cabin's owner's had asked if I would take care of their cockatiel. His name was something like Billy or Tweety or God-knows-what, but I of course renamed him Descartes, which seemed to me appropriately clever—it would make for a great conversation-starter, allowing me to impress visitors with my knowledge of philosophy, of which in reality I had very little.

That night I went to the restaurant, and all my hopes were confirmed. The owner was a jovial, accommodating, and very generous drunk. The bartender thought I was cool. The waitresses were pretty, aggressive, and absolutely thrilled to have a real live Rock Star Wannabe supposedly rehabbing in their little world. The entire staff seemed deeply committed to their collective alcoholism. I told jokes and funny stories about Hollywood and made everyone laugh. I sang songs, and the girls swooned. Long after the doors were closed and locked, we sat around the bar like life-long friends catching up on things. It was almost as if everyone considered me the returning hero, back in my home village following the Great Crusade.

Well, well—I thought—*Things are looking up. Maybe this is home.*

This charade went on for months. Remarkably, the people loved me, though they were admittedly starved for quality entertainment. I was now a bigger fish in a much smaller pond, and that suited me fine.

Since I only had to work Thursdays through Saturdays, there was much time to engage in some of the things I loved, like reading and writing. I did little of either. Mostly, I fine-honed my drug and alcohol use, drawing the local dopers to me like a magnet. I sat on my back porch and smoked weed, and thought deep narcissistic thoughts. I planned great books in my head. I languished in the illusion of some true purpose—a well-loved poet-drunk, sort of a local Dylan Thomas, cynical, romantically pitiable, yet deserving of much measured respect.

At night, I began methodically moving from one "romance" to another. Courtship was not a prerequisite. They were eager to please. The town subsisted on tourists, but we "insiders" survived within our own small-minded subculture. In L.A., I had girlfriends spread out all over the expansive territory, following the "warm hearth in every port" theory of intimacy, without any of them ever being aware of the other. Here, though, it was all one big happy family, and we changed partners as we would our socks, passing ourselves around like half-burnt joints.

One night, a stranger came into the bar. She sat down at a little table near my piano, and watched me sing. I noticed her immediately—tall, delicate, long brown hair. She was pretty, but not extraordinarily so, with an honest face and ease of manner. She wasn't all that striking from a distance, but she was new, and I watched her watching me.

After the set, I asked if I could sit with her, and she said yes.

"You sing beautifully," she said. And sitting this close, I realized how strange her eyes looked, liquid and green as the sea. They sat in her placid, somewhat plain face like two enormous painted planets, teeming with life. And her voice was bright and infectious, without the least hint of pretense.

"Do you live here?" I asked, trying to sound interested, though in reality I was sizing up just how easily she might be seduced.

She looked at me as if I had asked something utterly ridiculous. "No. I'm just visiting," she said finally. "I like to travel."

We talked for the entire break. I leaned back in my chair and did my best to impress, by now a fairly refined act, when I was sober enough. I noticed she wasn't drinking at all.

"How long will you be in Alpine Lake?" I asked.

"You never know," she said.

I flirted some more, and she smiled at me as if I were very odd, watching me with a sort of curiosity, and occasionally a look came in to her watery eyes that reflected something a little like kindness and sadness all mixed together. She seemed both deeply interested and completely unimpressed, and I found this both intriguing and disconcerting. I asked if she'd like to stay around with me after we'd closed and have a drink. She declined, politely, and at some point during my last set, I noticed she had gone.

Descartes liked to sit on my shoulder. One wing had been clipped, and although he could flap his feathers fast enough to keep from hurting himself in a fall, he couldn't fly too high or too far, and was content to spend much of his time riding along with me throughout the cabin, chirping in my ear, his little claws digging into my shirt. I believed Descartes added to my eccentric image. I thought—*How very interesting I must appear, here in my self-imposed isolation, music up loud, bird droppings on my sleeve.* Over time, I taught Descartes to wolf-whistle, which delighted and amused all my female visitors.

One morning, the girl with the pale green eyes knocked on my cabin door.

"Hello, Jim." *She remembered my name.*

"Hi," I said.

"You don't remember my name, do you?"

"Sure I do," I lied.

"No, you don't," she said, with her small, almost-sad smile.

She came in, looked at me, and then around the cabin. We were both a mess.

"It's not much," I said with appropriate false bravado, "but it's home."

"I see." That's what she said. *I see. What an odd person.*

"I've come to ask if you'd like to fly," she said finally.

Descartes sat on my shoulder, and we both stared at her.

"I'd like to take you flying," she said, looking me right in the eye.

"Don't tell me," I said. "You're a pilot?"

"Yes," she said. Then: "Tonight?"

She showed up halfway through my last set. I still thought she was kidding, of course. But at least she seemed interested in being with me. I could probably score, if I went along with the game.

Later, she drove us to the little airfield, which wasn't much more than a stretch of partially-paved land, and a few seemingly random landing lights, flashing eerily, suspended low along the shadows. Even as we pulled up near the two-seater Cessna, which sat somewhat isolated from a handful of other planes near aluminum hangars, I kept expecting her to finally let me in on the gag. The place looked abandoned. Where were all the official-looking people, the ones who knew what they were doing? The whole scene slightly unnerved me: this fragile girl now hopping from the car, confident and in control, methodically inspecting the plane, sliding up into the pilot seat, acting as if she had done this sort of thing a hundred

times. After a moment, I realized we really were going to
fly. I got out of the car, holding my whiskey bottle.

"Can I bring this?" I asked. Then, in my W. C. Fields
voice—"I say, little girl, I'm not leaving planet earth without this." Ha Ha.

She looked towards me, there in the near-darkness. I
couldn't see her eyes.

"It doesn't matter if you bring it or not," she said.

Up. Off the paved runway and up, gently, side by side in
the little cockpit, straight toward the moon. I watched
her. She looked almost absurd, the headset wrapped
around her soft hair, the delicate hands holding us aloft
with light, casual movements of the controls. A part of me
thought about being scared, just for a moment, because I
had no idea who this person was or how in the world I'd
suddenly ended up in an airplane with her. I tried being
funny, showing my mock bravery by making one asinine
comment after another. But she remained quiet, and after
a while I stopped trying. I thought of clever things to say,
but decided not to say them.

We flew in quiet astonishment through the night. The
sky was black and clear, and we rose up among the stars and
looked down on the shrinking mountains. The moon, nearly
full, was bright enough to illuminate us, the plane, the whole
earth. We flew like this for a while, finally crossing over a
series of ridges jutting out from the blanket of treetops.

Then, into another galaxy. Below us lay an alien
world. We were above a dry lakebed—a flat, bare expanse,

seemingly miles and miles of it, like some abandoned excavation site, or a place cleared away for a civilization that never evolved. And then we began sinking, lightly drifting down toward a prehistoric land, the eerie surface rising up to meet us. I looked at her, and she was all calm and control.

She was going to land. On the lakebed. I wanted to say something like—*Do you think this is safe? Have you done this before?* But I sat still and mute, not breathing.

And we touched down, gently, rolling along the wrinkled clay in bright, bright moonlight, bright enough to cast a hard shadow of the plane onto the weird world around us. When she cut the engine, the silence was almost terrifying. The two of us, so near the stars, close enough to almost touch them, and not another soul in existence.

We got out of the plane. I stepped onto the chalky surface, wondering if it would even support my weight. The barren land lay out lifelessly, eternally, smooth and endless, its round edge cutting finally into the blackest of horizons. I felt as if we stood frozen in deep space, upon the surface of an asteroid, or a pale, parched planet. Negligible, we crawled like fleas across the cracked and creviced hide of some enormous, sleeping animal.

After walking a short distance, I turned and looked at the plane; it sat there like a pitiful, plastic model barely held together with glue—miniscule and insignificant, weightless, and fatally fragile. The frost plumes of our breath hung heavy and long in the air, like little clouds caught in a vacuum, and I realized how small we were, and vulnerable, how we would never survive the night should the little toy engine refuse to start again. But I felt too stunned to be afraid. Everything was washed in one indescribable color, a monochrome of silver and blue and gray and yet none of those things, as if the cool light coating us and our new world in soft powder was originating from another sun, reflecting off an alien moon.

"How do you like it?" she asked, softly, her voice an endless, echoing whisper.

I could not speak.

I don't know how long we stayed there. Time had changed. And all other thoughts went away, into space, cold and empty—thoughts of seducing her, of using and abandoning, of medicating. *I can't hide here,* I thought. *I can't disappear, here in the open, so exposed, so small.* Dizzy, I sat down unsteadily in the gray clay, hard and dimpled as rhinoceros skin, suddenly unsure, as if everything—me, her, the whole weightless world beneath us—might float away and be forever lost. And she sat beside me, this strange stranger, bundled in a coat and scarf, and we stared together at the steely stars, at the cosmos just beyond our fingertips.

And then, she said this: "The light will come back."

I did not feel drunk or sober, thirsty or satisfied. I felt insignificant and of great consequence, meaningless and substantial. Humbled, frightened, awed. Lost, but watched. I did not know who this person was, or understand what she was saying. But her words were sure and clear as the night, her small, soft voice rumbling like thunder through the stunned silence. I knew then that although she and I would never touch in the hungry, helpless way I had grown accustomed to, we were in this fantasy suddenly connecting, our faces flush against the heavens...*her eyes, my eyes*...our bodies turned to iridescent dust, here in this foreign yet familiar place high on a mountaintop.

A single moment might have passed, or a million years. Then, she reached out her hand through the white, glowing mist, and very gently touched my cheek. And, deep and distant within me, I knew that this space in time had little to do with us, really...*this fragile, indestructible, unexplainable moment brushing by us like a soft hand against our wondering faces...a mother's hand...God's hand...*

"The Light will come back to you," she said, her voice less than real and more than human, coming from far away, out of the endless emptiness, both of us shimmering there in the cold fire of the moon.

And there we paused, suspended, listening together to the still, silent singing of angels.

The next morning, I woke in my cabin, alone, trying to remember. I knew it had happened, but it still didn't seem real. And, in fact, though I didn't know it at the time, I would never see the girl again. Some would say later that she left for Colorado, where she lived, though others said they thought she had mentioned Canada. No one seemed to know for sure.

Not bothering to shower, I pulled on some dirty clothes and opened a beer. I took Descartes out of his cage, and rode him on my shoulder to the back deck, just like every morning. As I bent to sit, he startled—only now, he didn't just float harmlessly down a few feet away. Time, patient and imperceptible, had given him new wings. He moved forward on the air, testing, then furiously flapping he rose a bit, hanging there, and pushed his way higher, then higher still. I stood and stared, fascinated, my hand reaching out to him as if there were a string attached...and, suspended for one final moment, his little black eyes shining with something between panic and ecstasy, he chose. I could only watch, silently mouthing his name, as he slowly disappeared into the towering pines, yellow head flashing in the sunlight.

All morning, I tried everything: putting his cage outside, sprinkling his food all over the deck railing. I sat for the rest of the afternoon, wolf-whistling. It was, all in all, a helpless feeling, my being earthbound again.

For a while, a sadness fell over me. At that altitude, it wasn't uncommon for the temperature to drop more than forty degrees from day to night, and I knew he wouldn't survive. As I continued drinking, though, the warm sun passing slowly through the sky, then melting away into dusk, I began to view things more philosophically. Sipping thoughtfully, I did what I did best, romanticizing the loss. Pondering the hidden recesses of the treetops, and the deepening purple clouds beyond, I blurredly imagined the little gray bird as a kind of Noble Seeker, lifted on the wings of some false but tantalizing Truth toward a lofty ambition worthy of bird-martyrdom. I saw that he had unexpectedly come upon his own proverbial two roads diverged in a wood, suspended there in that moment between my hand and the sky, and had by nature been forced to decide. And his choice, of course, would make all the difference. Maybe what he was to find up there would, however briefly, prove worth the sacrifice of being turned into a frozen, feathered popsicle. Either way, it seemed to me that Descartes had risen up on dreams of his own making, above and beyond the confinements of his existence, and that he would at least die with his heart racing, wide eyes cast out onto the immensity of Creation.

Alas, Shangri-La was not to be. It lasted less than a year. Gradually, I became more tiresome than entertaining to those around me; my quick admittance into the inner circle would be followed by just as quick an exit. Everybody knew everybody else's secrets in the little place, and my secrets were, even in this hedonistic environment, increasingly scandalous. Although the drunk owner still found me amusing, I had insulted one too many customers, and sat in one too many married lady's lap—with the husband staring aghast, there in a room full of people eating lobster tails and drinking Chardonnay.

I didn't want to go back to L.A., but felt I had nowhere else to go. My patron-of-the-arts friend expressed her disappointment that the restaurant gig hadn't worked out, and offered to let me stay in a little rental property she owned, at least for a while, so I knew I'd have a roof over my head. And I knew Emilia would also be there, waiting. But a deep sense of failure and dominating despair had overwhelmed me by now. I felt as though I'd destroyed yet another thing I'd touched, and that people hated me, although not nearly so much as I hated myself.

Coming down the mountain, I didn't know who was left there in the desert for me to cheat. But down I went just the same, empty, returning through the red haze, turning and running like some poor dumb animal, back into a burning building.

the screeching of bats

Baja, Mexico. *This place is stranger even than* L.A., *weirder than being a flea on the back of some monster moon, and comforting to me somehow. I find myself here again, in this most bizarre of worlds—the middle of the day already filled with drunks and crazies, shooting tequila and dancing on the tables...music coming from the street, barn-like doors open on both ends of the building...sweltering heat and sweat, flies perched drunkenly on the rim of my shot glass, mange-eaten dogs running under the tables searching for scraps. I sit alone, very still, watching a wasp slowly beating itself to death against the window, again and again... tap, tap, tap. Later, when the sun sinks lower over the dirt-dry streets, the prostitutes will appear, apparitions working the room, all red rouge and black widow lashes, leading willing victims by the hand to the flea-infested rooms upstairs...*

"Ah, es mi amigo gringo loco,"—a tug on my pants under the table, and looking down I see a man with no legs, sitting on a square wooden platform with wheels screwed into the bottom. Every day he is here, pulling himself with his hands across the filthy floor, table to table, and he knows me now. "¿ Se siente usted el hoy valiente?" he squeaks, knowing I can never turn him down. I mumble that I am brave enough, and return my gaze to the wasp. Then, another tug. "Are you a macho man today, my friend?" he asks, and I blink, and look down at him— grimy-faced and nearly toothless, one eye a white marble, holding out to me two metal cylinders, each with coiled wires on one end connected to what looks something like a car battery sitting where his legs should be. "Are you a real man, Señor?" And someone brings me another shot of mezcal, with the fabled hallucinogenic grub lying in the bottom of the glass. And I do not hesitate, gulping it down worm and all, then hand him his crumpled pesos and take a rod in each hand. Slowly, grinning, he turns a dial on the battery, increasing the voltage little by little, a small crowd gathering around, cheering me on... the charge slowly building and coursing through me until my hands are on fire, my arms numb, sparks shooting behind my clenched eyelids...

Shock treatment.
Not letting go...not letting go...

I became obsessed with doing "brave" things. I spent time in dangerous places, with dangerous people. Desperately desiring to be courageous, I would accept almost any challenge. One morning, I drank two quarts of beer before the sun was up and climbed aboard a crop duster bi-plane, the nut-case pilot having taunted me in a bar the night before, claiming I couldn't handle it. He sat in the only seat, and I crawled up behind him, one leg shoved down behind his back, my butt hanging off the side, holding on to the wing supports. He took me under telephone lines, mere feet from the ground, into power dives, insane air stunts, everything he could muster to make me cry for mercy. This was the opposite of my midnight flight to the moon—all ear-shattering volume and violence and vibration, more rape than rapture. And I held on, terrified but silent, refusing to give in, and when he finally landed in the dirt field I crawled off the plane and walked away, trying not to collapse, faking a smile.

"You've got guts!" he yelled, a cigar hanging from his mouth.

But I knew he was wrong.

The death of one's spirit is agonizingly slow. Lying there on the ground with the dirt in my eyes and the rope seemingly far out of reach, I did not call out for Him. Though He

198 Prodigal Song: A Memoir

was all and everything that was missing, I could no longer remember His name. Some part of me had become buried, deceived and blind, and the child who had once called Him friend could not now recognize Him at all. I was alone, and that seemed right, because I had finally accepted myself as something loathsome and wretched and unlovable, a terrible emptiness feeding on what was left of me, distancing me from the only One who could save me.

I don't know how it happens. We get lost. We suddenly find ourselves seeking escape from a life that had once been a natural celebration, the child in us changing into something frightened and miserable, obsessed with finding a way out, a door through, until somehow we arrive at this place of shadows and dread, this dead end journey into self that eats away at us, not knowing until much too late just how far we've wandered away.

And so, without His air to breath or His food to eat, the weeks turned to months turned to years turned to ashes, no more dreams and no more laughter and no more life. Finally. Finally the gas was gone and the car stalled and the dark so deep I knew there was no hope of ever walking out of the woods.

All I really wanted, I think, all I *really* wanted was to die. I don't know how I reached that place, when the exhilaration of adventure turned into despair. I suppose the darkness had always been within me, like a mushroom down in the cellar, hidden but all the while growing beneath the soil. All I know is that somehow, almost without my being aware, the brightness inside me had cooled and was nearly out. The fire that had brought me so far was now nothing more than a glowing coal, and I hid in my haze, waiting for something to snuff it out.

Sitting in the waiting area, reading a magazine. She sits beside me, silent and removed. When they call her name, she looks at me, just for a moment, and I can't tell what is in her eyes. She stares at me, wearily, as if something barely held together within her has finally broken, as though something has changed her mind, changed her heart, if only for an instant. Maybe she is reconsidering. Maybe she wants me to do something, to tell her I've changed my mind, too, that I want to be with her no matter what, that we can live together and be more, be...what...a family? I don't say anything, just squeeze her hand a little, and try to smile. It's amazing, really, that I'm sobered up enough to be here with her at all. And her look realizes, gives up, and from that moment on she would never look at me quite the same. There is no anger in her face, or resentment, even. Just a faint sadness, resignation, a small yet sure emptiness I had never seen before... as if, at that very moment, she had lost all that was left of her love for me. And then someone calls out her name, and she follows the nurse through a door.

Later, she doesn't seem to be in any real pain, more uncomfortable and sleepy than anything else. I've helped put her in bed, asked if there is anything she needs before I go. "Stay with me," she is saying. "You don't have to leave," and I know that she is right, and wrong. "Stay," she says, but by now she has given up, dropped her outstretched hand, looking away from me and towards the window.

"I'll be back," I say, and I have no idea if it is true or not...

～～

So much of it, I simply can't recall. There's nothing left but flashes of memory, mercifully unclear. And yet some of the images that sneak through are too dark and sordid to tell, without giving evil more sensational coverage than it deserves. Or maybe I'm still just too ashamed.

But I remember clearly the day, there in my empty apartment—the phone ringing, my heart pounding, and a few moments later numbly pulling down my suitcase from the closet shelf. Twenty-eight years old, long-hidden from the responsibilities of my far away family, wrapped so tightly around myself that I could often fool that self into thinking there was no real tragedy playing out all those thousands of miles away. But here it came rushing back.

After one earlier attempt, this time she had succeeded. After being dead in her spirit for so long, after divorce and being left lonely and bitter and with no one close to minister to her, my mother had finally found a way, finally taken enough pills and washed them down with enough booze, though the doctors said her heart was still barely beating. She was almost done dying, now, broken into too many pieces, and though I had been trying to hide from her, and from what she had become and what I had become and what my family had become, suddenly the selfish insulation around me crumbled, just for a moment, and reality crashed down.

And I was packing to fly home, knowing that she was all but dead, knowing evil had killed her, that darkness can seemingly win, and that I had only *thought* I had been hiding, because she had never been far from my heart, cold and empty as it was. I knew then that suicide was possible, and that my prophesy of self-destruction would surely one day come to pass, as it always does when, cut off from our source of life, we finally wither and die.

But even this didn't wake me. I sleep-walked, floating down the hospital hallway like a ghost, the blue fluorescent lights humming overhead, the ICU machines hissing and sucking like some mortally wounded animal gasping for air. None of it seemed real, none of it could break through my shell, dig into the deep of me. Not even the sight of her, this young woman turned suddenly ancient, bloated and yellow with jaundice, skin the color of old paper, lips pulled back over her teeth and mouth locked in a silent howl on her skeleton face...*and I knew in an instant that she was not there.* I could have reached across the space between us and touched her, lying there in those last moments with the tubes coming out, *and it wouldn't have changed a thing.* She was not there, and neither was I—not even when she opened her eyes and saw me, shocked, startling me, as if this brief return from near-death had unexpectedly brought her face to face with someone she had been dreaming about.

"Jimmy?" she tried to say, but there was no sound. Her eyes, helpless, like the eyes of someone falling, reaching..."*Jimmy.*" And then, as if convinced I was only a dream and nothing more, gone. It was the last time I ever saw her.

That night in my hotel room, I sat at the foot of the bed, inches from the TV screen, smoking a joint, watching some comedy show. I laughed so hard, tears rolled down my face.

The next day I would help bury my mother, going through the motions of responsibility, standing at the edge of the pit, the casket slowly sinking down. Although everyone at the funeral home had done their best to make her look if not peaceful then at least presentable, her body was too much ravaged, and for the service we had decided to keep the casket closed. Now, at the graveside, we all gathered and watched her go.

My father stood there, stone-faced and silent, perhaps so wearied and removed from it all that he could no longer feel much of anything, still emotionally absent as he had been all along. He and I had not spoken much to one another in some time, certainly nothing very meaningful. I felt too ashamed to let him get a really good look at me. I suppose both of us felt as if we had abandoned one another, which of course we had, and I guess a part of me had for a very long time been still waiting for him to rescue us, waiting for him to do something heroic, something remarkable, like hitting a home run left-handed over the Rexall Drug fence. I wanted him to be strong and fearless, to chase away the bad guys, to arrive like the cavalry at the last possible moment and save the day. But on this day, out of the corner of my eye, I saw just a man, someone no less lost and bewildered than the rest of us, with perhaps no Father of his own to call for help. He looked as if he felt nothing.

I was high, of course, standing there in my borrowed black suit beside my sisters, bloodshot eyes hidden behind dark glasses, wondering if *I* were supposed to be feeling anything, either—anything other than fear, than a desire to get away to a place much more distant than California, to a place far off the planet where no one could ever hope to reach. I felt something else, too, and with it even more shame. I felt relief. Not that she had gone, but that I would no longer have to deal with the guilt of not wanting to be near her, to help her. Of no longer having to look into her heartbreakingly sad eyes and seeing trapped inside the young and beautiful girl she had always been to me, bright and golden and laughing. I stood there, stoned, staring down into that hole in the ground, oblivious to the reality of it, feeling as little as I possibly could.

"It's a very sad time," Mamaw was saying, drying her eyes with one of her hand-sewn handkerchiefs. "Our sweet little Mary Jo," she said, and I wanted to hold her close, but did not, not wanting her to smell my breath, not wanting to feel what she was feeling. Sitting in her green chair, the one she had always sat in when I performed for her, looking much older now, and more tired. She suddenly gazed right into me.

"All those things she said, and did," Mamaw spoke softly, gently, as if I were a child, "she didn't mean it, Jimmy. She wasn't our Mary Jo...our sweet Mary Jo..."

And I didn't—couldn't—answer, just sat there across the room, hands on my knees, wanting to run. She looked at me, and saw me. Her eyes said many things. I stared down at the floor.

After a moment, Mamaw straightened a bit, and said, "Papaw would love to see you before you say good-bye." I stood up and walked into the bedroom.

The picture of Jesus hung on the wall, His eyes appearing to look somewhere else. Mamaw was keeping her promise; Papaw didn't want to die in a hospital. How she got him dressed and cleaned and fed every day all by herself I'll never know. My dad and sisters tried to help as much as they could. But Mamaw never complained. She wanted to take care of him, just as she had always done. The rented hospital bed was pulled over near a window so that Papaw could look outside, though none of us could be sure if he knew what he saw. A cool breeze was blowing through the screen, gently lifting the white sheer curtains.

Standing next to him, *looking down*. He appeared tiny, his legs drawn up like a baby's, eyes closed, eyelids lightly dancing. I wanted to leave, and just let him dream. But then his eyes opened, slowly, and for a moment he tried to focus on the ceiling, then turned his head toward me. His face showed nothing at first, then a spark, then that tooth-less grin gradually crept across his face. He made a sound in his throat, a held note, like the beginning of a word, or a song. I reached out, awkwardly, and put my hand on his.

"Hello, Papaw," I said, and his eyes looked right into mine, that squished-sparkly look in them, as if he were on two strong legs again, standing near the edge of laughter.

He kept making that sound, that low almost-humming, and the afternoon sun shone through the trees and cast dancing leaves on the walls around us.

Come waltz me around again Willie...Around, around, around...

And Mamaw, who had been standing just behind me, lightly touched my shoulder, like a friend about to share some secret, then silently turned and left the room, closing the door behind her.

A long and still moment hovered over us...*Come waltz me around again, Willie...*my trembling hand covering the wrinkled brown leather of his...a sweet stare, soft and relentless, boring into me like kind, cool fire, holding me there, helpless...*Around, around, around...*something coming up at me, from within me, from nowhere, somewhere...*Come waltz me around again, Willie...*until I couldn't see and the room was washed away, the silent tears coming, my body shaking, leaning down with my lips to his ear, softly...

"I liked that go-kart, Papaw," I said.

I went back to L.A., as quickly as possible, the engines of the jet roaring, the little bottles of bourbon lining up on the tray in front of me, my face against the window, every mile drugging and lulling me back, back, returning to the land of Make Believe to finish the destruction.

And from up there, helplessly hanging between heaven and earth, the barely-rippled clouds spread out far and forever below like endless miles of freshly fallen snow.

"You can't love anything," she is saying, the sheets pulled up under her chin, despite the hellish heat. I have come back to her again, drawn now more by helplessness than hope. We've been lying there for a while, silent, vacant. The ceiling fan is going full speed, pushing the heat around us…the black blades spinning, spinning…outside, a mournful wailing, the insatiable sirens screaming in the streets. "All you do is use people," she says, her voice as dry as the desert air—"You can't give me anything, can you?"—and I hear her as from miles away, droning and distant and meaningless, the sweat going into my eyes. And then something like—"You make me feel so empty"—and she's out of bed, getting dressed, leaving, the door closing. And I feel both afraid and affirmed, somehow knowing it's the last time…

I did not want to live, imprisoned this way. I knew how it would end, and the sadness of it caved in on me and finished me, choking out hope. And yet, the breath moved in and out of me, and time passed, month after long month. Nothing could save me, I knew that.

Not even, finally, losing my dearest friend. After two long years of suffering in that rest home, now Mamaw was gone, too. On what I thought would be my final trip to Tennessee, I could do no more than stand there staring, powerless. She lay quivering, a tube feeding her stomach, eyes open in some sort of fear-stare, a little girl wanting to run, to ride a bike, to *fly* out of that damned place, out of that broken body, wordlessly moving her lips...*help me, save me...*

I tried to tell her. But by then I had waited too long, and it seemed too late, so filled with fear that it was all I could do to make myself go and be with her. I held my breath against the sharp, stale-sick smell of that room, the blank stare, the semi-consciousness, as if both of us were in the middle of some terrible dream and couldn't wake up. I stood helplessly at the foot of her bed, incredulous, her thin hair matted back, lips cracked open. Her eyes horrified me. They stared at the ceiling and never seemed to rest, open wide as if she were perpetually shocked at what had happened to her. The only sounds she made were like the whimpering of a frightened child. I felt sure that she needed me to sit beside the bed and stroke her hair and read to her, sing for her. I blinked back tears and tried to tell her why I had gone, *where* I had gone, but the words choked me, and I turned my head and chewed at the inside of my cheek until I tasted blood. Lost in my own self-loathing, I couldn't comfort her the way she had comforted me as a child. And so my spirit stood paralyzed, in that place smelling of vomit and stale death, unable to look and unwilling to leave, there with her and yet not with her at all. Finally I snuck away, miserable and defeated, not knowing enough to recognize the possible gift in it, the God in it, this chance to be for her what she had always been for me. This chance to say thank you. This chance to say goodbye.

Strangely, it was during this terrible time that I remember praying. For the first time in forever I turned and spoke—*Why are you doing this? How can you treat her this way?*—a miserable prayer, full of anger and silent shouting, but a prayer just the same. *DAMN YOU! WHAT KIND OF GOD ARE YOU?* I screamed in my head, shaking my fist at the empty sky, more convinced than ever that He was not there. And yet I couldn't help shouting His name.

When she finally died, again came a feeling of great relief. I wouldn't have to feel guilty about not visiting anymore. I tried very hard not to think about her dying alone.

She left what few things she had to her three grandchildren; for me, an old clock and an AM radio. And she wanted me to have the spindle bed, though I had no place to keep it, so Joette promised to store it for me in her basement. And I got a shoebox, taped shut.

I didn't open it until I had returned to Los Angeles. Sitting by the window in my apartment, the sun slowly surrendering into a rust-red haze, I pulled off the tape. Inside were some old photographs, and Papaw's handkerchiefs and pocketknives, a few scraps of paper with some of my first poems, and a silver dollar. And a very old Bible with Mamaw's name written on the inside cover. And then I saw something else, and felt a small strange shudder. It was my little picture, the one of the white dove. I held it in the palm of my hand, and stared at it for a long time, the room growing dim around me. In the bottom right hand corner, in tiny print, I noticed something I hadn't remembered.

Psalm 55: 4–6

Without thinking, I immediately opened her Bible, turned through the brown pages, and found the place.

My heart is in anguish within me,
And the terrors of death
have fallen upon me.
Fear and trembling come upon me;
And horror has overwhelmed me.
And I said,
"Oh, that I had wings like a dove!
I would fly away and be at rest."

Back into the night, waiting for the wounds to do me in, for it all to mercifully end. The emptiness, the thirsting. A fifth-and-a-half a day blackout drunk, morning to night, drinking now just to stave off the panic attacks and seizures, even my waking moments no more than a continuing, terrible nightmare. Homeless in body and soul, time passing like one long and sleepless night, in the mirror now slumped someone almost unrecognizable, worshipping fear, existence slowed and blurred into a sort of dull amnesia. Shades pulled, towels stuffed under the door, a paranoid, seamless time of nothingness, with no day or night…lost in the ice-silent sound of sanity slipping away.

A still small voice spake unto me—wrote Tennyson—
Thou art so full of misery / Were it not better not to be?

I know now that I hovered near death many times, unconscious following a binge, reliving the same nightmare, again and again. My mind, my *spirit* would try to wake up, but couldn't, trapped inside my own dead corpse. I would try to speak, try to move and roll over and off the bed onto the floor in a desperate attempt to startle myself into consciousness, silently screaming for help, as if my soul were hurling itself against the walls of my passed-out body, trying to escape. And then, always, a *real* scream and violent jerk awake, the sheets soaked with sweat, heart pounding, gasping…knowing how close I must have been, enough booze in me to kill two men, how close my heart must have been to stopping before something had let me come back one more time.

I've dreams and years past resurrection;
a soul that nothing can renew…
—*ALEXANDER PUSHKIN*

And I'm climbing that hill again, alone this time. It's tough going with only one free hand, but I'm not about to surrender the half-empty bottle cradled at my side…*not letting go…not letting go*…and it's up ten feet and sliding down fifteen, scraping my knees and elbows, cursing the hill, the night, the mean and meaningless night, until finally somehow I'm there, blinking up at the thing. The memory is badly blurred—I think I must have been trying to climb the H again, but there was no one to lift me up— and I fall flat on my ass into the weeds and crumpled beer cans, my back against the crumbling monument, our glory days gone, a fallen king amid the rubble. I shake my head and try to focus, staring out at the city through the rusty haze hanging heavy over it like smoke following a bombing, dull and colorless and lifeless.

And from somewhere far away, the sound of separate sirens crying out, lonesome as wolves...

I am dreaming. And my mother is sitting in a chair next to my bed. She is dressed for church, her hair curled and piled high on her head. She is young and shining and beautiful, no more than a young girl, and I'm filled with great joy and relief to see her this way, to know that it's all been some awful misunderstanding up till now, and that things are going to be okay again. And she smiles at me, and all my pain eases, and tears of joy begin to run down my face, and I know now all of this is real, that I needn't ever wake up, because I can taste the salt of my tears. And then, as I reach out my hand toward her face, her smile suddenly fades around these words—"We're going to the funeral home, honey"—and my hand stops mid-way, her face changing, withering, the skin pulling back around her cheekbones, eyes turning black as a storm cloud— "We're going to the funeral home to say goodbye..."

And I'm running, running as fast as I can, and my feet are heavy, ankle-deep in something thick, like mud, but bright blood-red, and the muscles in my legs are on fire...being chased, whatever it is close behind me snorting hot, smelly breath on my neck...and then I'm falling from a ledge, heart bursting, my eyes clamped together against the coming collision, praying this time it kills me ...

My eyes open. My bones and head pound. I feel crushed by the impact, but there has been no impact. And then the slow realization that I'm in a cell, curled up, lying on a metal rack attached to the wall. There is no mattress, just a flat slab with holes in it. Through the bars I see a bare light bulb hanging from a wire in the passageway ceiling. I don't know if it's day or night. I can't move my arms or legs at first, so I start by trying to wiggle my toes and fingers, and slowly the blood gets back into them—then, fire shooting up from my right knee. My tongue is stuck to the roof of my mouth. I touch my face, and feel my upper lip, swollen, split open. I have the faintest sense of a memory, an image of someone hitting me.

And then, from the cell next to me, an unseen voice in the damp darkness—*Jingle Baa-ills...Jingle Baa-ills...Jingle all da waaaay*—still drunk as a skunk and obviously feeling no pain, his voice slurred and goofy—*oooooh wut fuuun...it is to riiiide*...and then a fierce shaking of the bars, the clanging echoing down the corridor and straight into my burning brain. I can feel the nausea rising up from my stomach into my throat, and then the singer screams—*Heeeey, let me outta heeeere*...and I try to concentrate past the pain, try to move my head, but it's all gray darkness and cold sweating metal, and the stench of a filthy toilet bolted to the back wall...*SHUT UP IN THERE!*—a guard's angry voice, and the rattling stops for a moment. And though I have no idea exactly where I am or how I got there, I suddenly realize for certain and for no good reason that it's Thanksgiving Day.

Jingle Baa-ills, Jingle Baa-ills...

STOP SINGIN' THAT SONG OR I'M COMIN' IN THERE AND SHUTTIN' YOU UP! And then silence, for maybe a minute. Then—

OOOOHHH...*Here comes Santie Clause, Here comes Santie Clause, Right down Santie Clause laaaaaane!*

∽◦∾

Fear of death will never stop the addict. It is, in some twisted way, death that we seek. Lost jobs, lost relationships, *lost.* The way always grows darker still. One too many wild turns, the roads becoming paths then trails then nothing but woods, and the shouted directions more and more meaningless until we find ourselves in places once unimaginable...waking from some wordless agony on a beach in Mexico, face down, mouth full of sand, no idea where I was or how I had gotten there...the dark and morbid back rooms of crack houses, rail-thin men huddled around like zombies, black-skinned and sallow-eyed, eerie shadows leaping from a single candle on the table, the gun lying there inches from the dope and the pipe and the snake-like hiss of the butane torch, roaches crawling off the walls and over my shoes...the time spent in jail, dull damp drunk-tanks smelling of mold and urine and puke. The horrible non-life of shame, howling through the night like some wounded animal, coming to before dawn, naked on the floor with one eye black and swollen shut, the wine bottles lying around me like crash victims, the last of their blood dripping out and staining the rug. And then one night the world is no more, and we are no more, and there is nothing left of us but the shrill sirens ripping a gash through our souls...barricaded in the back room, a dresser dragged in front of the door, going mad, laughing and crying and begging for mercy...curled up in the corner, hiding from the enemy, from the creatures outside drawing their curved claws across the windows, screeching like bats. Hands shaking, licking the phantom remains of cocaine from the filthy mirror, and seeing there a blurred madness reflected back in the eyes of some demented stranger, peering at me from a place called hell. And knowing, in that moment, that the waiting was over.

I was already dead.

nearing home

"After he had spent everything,
there was a severe famine
in that whole country,
and he began to be in need...
He longed to fill his stomach
with the pods that the pigs
were eating, but no one
gave him anything."
—*LUKE 15: 14, 16*

Something smells bad,
and I think it's me.
—*MARY RUTH ROBINSON (AGE FOUR)*

floating

December, 1988

There is nothing more written on the back of this one. It wasn't in the box; I found it packed away with some of my few remaining possessions from back then. The handwriting is not my own. I have no memory of who took the picture, and there are no clues to help identify where it was taken. A bar, maybe. Staring at it, I can barely recognize myself.

I'm sitting in a chair, smiling maniacally, drink in hand, the background dark and out of focus. Thirty pounds overweight, my face red and splotchy, eyes puffed up like someone who's been in a fistfight. And there is no light in them at all...

Alone. Those who have been there know what kind of place it is: a separation, a solitude that has nothing to do with the physical world around you, a spiritual disease of utter emptiness, an unshakable feeling of never fitting in, never belonging, always peering out at a strange and foreign world from within the unlit sanctuary of our *selves*.

"*How long, O Lord?*" sang David in his own song of sorrow. "*Wilt thou forget me forever? How long wilt thou hide Thy face from me?*" Many of us find ourselves lost without the aid of drugs; we lose someone we love very much, or we become exhausted caring for someone who is sick, or perhaps we're just born with something wired wrong in our heads, but for whatever reason we can't seem to join in and be part of living, and so instead become part of dying. "*How long must I bear pain in my soul...*" And though our methods of transportation may differ, the destination is always the same: without His touch, we live in a hell on earth.

"*Look on me and answer, O Lord my God...*"

Small voices crying into the night, no longer believing in the dawn, unaware of how near the song of morning waits.

"*Lighten my eyes, lest I sleep the sleep of death...*"

∽∾∾

Fast forward: A man, or what is left of him, now a desperate drunk, with no car, no job, no place to call home. I sold or gave away what few possessions I had left, keeping only enough to fill two backpacks, borrowed more money, and in one last vain attempt to run away bought an airplane ticket to London.

It wasn't far enough, of course. I had thought that maybe, just maybe, people would better understand me in Europe. A lot of my literary heroes had spent time there, after all. It struck me as a more civilized place, more artistic. Maybe I would fit in. My plan—the one in my head anyway—was to live there, and die there, after I had traveled some and discovered the country best suited for my poetic demise. Then, everyone would see me for who I truly was—a brilliant but terribly misunderstood genius, someone deserving their deep mourning, having burned brightly but oh so briefly. By this time, to use one of Papaw's colorful colloquialisms, I was nuttier than an outhouse rat.

But this plan got off to a bad start; severely hung over when I reached Gatwick, customs officials must have considered mine the face of a desperate and dangerous fellow. They detained me, and turned my two backpacks inside out. I had at least enough sense left in me not to have been carrying any drugs, but they still didn't like the looks of me, I guess, and eventually stamped my passport with a limited time restriction. I was in, but not for as long as I'd hoped.

I stayed in six-dollar hostels and cheap spare rooms in and around England, traveled by trains and ferries, walked miles and miles and drank my way through France and Italy. For the most part, the time was a waste—obscure recollections of London, of Paris and the islands of Greece, of long and languid days walking through the rural areas and countless small villages surrounded by rolling fields, sleeping in farmhouse rooms-for-rent and eating and drinking in dozens of pubs and taverns. Even though I traveled there the better part of seven months, the sad truth is that very few real memories remain with me now, numbed as I was to life, to living.

I sat one afternoon in the Roman Coliseum, and sleepwalked through a few ageless museums. One day, to escape the rain, I wandered into some ancient cathedral. Something small and bittersweet stirred in me as I entered, and with it the realization that I had not set foot inside a church for many years. A feeling both faint and familiar washed over me, cool and quiet. A few formless bodies, scattered and kneeling, low voices droning, near and distant...pleading, weeping, echoing off the domed mosaic covering me like sculpted sky, an immense canvas of blue and maroon, ancient, permanent, permeating. And I felt a thing inside me falling, crumpling to its knees under the weight of the murmured prayers, resisting, not quite surrendering to the heavy echoes coming hard into my heart. The breath wouldn't come into me, and I pushed past faceless bodies, searching for the door, filled more now with a deep uneasiness than awe, half-falling out into the false freedom of the street.

After that, I stayed mostly to the countryside.

I made no friends. As much as I had always longed to visit Europe, I stumbled through much of it more than half-blind, taking up space, dead to it all. And I discovered after a while that no matter how far I roamed my pain still clung to me, oppressive and inescapable, skulking after me like a shadow. I learned once more that there was no such thing as a geographical cure. The only thing left in my life I seemed to have the power to change was the scenery. And now most of that I can barely remember.

I traveled the whole length of Italy, perhaps the place I had always most wished to see. I went about as far as I could, down into the heel of the boot, and reaching the sea I looked out over its rolling expanse and wondered where else on earth I could possibly go.

A few days later—though I'm not really sure how many days had started or ended by then—while lying on a nearly deserted beach a few miles from the coastal town of Brindisi, I decided to kill myself. It wasn't some plotted, melodramatic moment; it came almost as an afterthought, something I had meant to do for the longest time but had somehow never quite gotten around to. I was so tired, so profoundly weary, that the thought of endless sleep brought with it a sort of resigned peace. Every indulgence had failed me. I felt finished. And so I stood up, almost casually, and walked into the green sea.

I swam out for some distance, to deep water that lay between huge boulders jutting out of the water like massive fists, blocking my view of the shore. I turned and floated on my back. I can't remember what I was thinking, if I was thinking anything at all. I suppose I expected to simply stop floating after a while and let the ocean have me, just let it pull me down and do away with me, once and for all. There was a peaceful, familiar moment when the ocean covered my ears, engulfing me in sweet silence. I closed my eyes. The sounds of the alien world were gone, leaving only the internal roar of my own breathing, in and out, and the pulse of blood through my body, echoing like a heartbeat in the womb. It all made sense, the salt of the sea, the salt of my tears. I lay there, feeling some sort of twisted satisfaction with my decision, not praying, not calling out. I simply let all the air out of my lungs and stopped trying to float...

And still I floated. Like an inflated inner tube, a life raft, easily and naturally, without any effort at all, as though unseen hands held me suspended, like a father's hands, teaching a child to trust the water. It was as though I could not for the death of me manage to sink. I must have bobbed there on the surface for half an hour, fascinated, but of course lacking the guts to actually force myself under the surface. Eventually I came back to shore. I don't remember what might have been going through my mind, if anything.

Later, in a bar, one of the English-speaking locals told me that the waters of the Adriatic Sea have a very high salt content, giving them unusual buoyancy.

Maybe so, I thought.

⮑⮏

I was running out of time, and money, but mostly I felt I had run out of room. Traveling back up through the middle of the country I made my way, by accident probably, into the old town streets of Verona. I arrived in the middle of the day, in the middle of the week, and yet the streets teamed with people, the place alive with celebration. Gold and purple banners flew above the buildings, and music drifted through the open doors of the shops. I tried asking some of the locals what was going on.

"This is...happy days," a man finally told me, walking along the street eating an ice cream cone. "We...play for the...soccer...champions...championsheeps...of all Italy. We are...how saying...very happy days." That afternoon their team would be competing in another city for the 1985 Italian league soccer championship. Since the league's formation in 1898, they had never won the championship (and have in fact never won it since). The village square was filled with booths and vendors. Posters of the team hung everywhere, and a PA system was blaring pregame festivities. Apparently no one had a TV set, because every last citizen seemed to be gathered outside, talking, gesturing, laughing, sprawled along the curbs and on the grass. Somehow, while in search of solitude, I'd stumbled into the biggest party the town had ever thrown.

I rented a room two stories above the square. Later that afternoon I tried milling around in the masses for a while. But the more I sank into the bustle and laughter of the crowd, the more isolated I felt, as if they were looking and walking right through me. I bought a bottle of Sambuca, went back to my room, and for the next few hours sat at the little table by my open window, watching. Hundreds of people gathered on the square, listening to the announcers. I couldn't understand a word, of course, but it was obvious when something good had happened for the home team—a hushed moment of silence, as if the entire town was holding its breath, followed by a huge roar and wild cheering. As the sun set, the game ended. Verona had won.

Long into the night I sat and watched, until the bottle was nearly gone. Little Fiat cars endlessly rounded the square, horns honking. People rode atop each other's shoulders, laughing and singing. I could hear their voices, the language they were speaking as alien to me as that of my own lost homeland. Floating above it all, I watched the dream-drama unfold, listening to their joy explode into the night sky like fireworks, flinching from the sparks of all these other lives that had nothing to do with my own, bound there in my room as the surreal procession passed under me again and again, a blurred circle of gold and purple, of flesh and blood and purpose, of relationship and meaning and living…one complete and fulfilled organism, undulating, joyful and understanding, lives bound together and inseparable, creatures born and reaching toward some unknown place but moving there *together,* very sure and very mortal, and yet somehow just out of my reach. I sat there with the windows open all night and into the ashen morning, unaffected and unattached, the great joy in the air unable to penetrate me, now something less than human and very much less than alive.

And there in my separate place, far away, well beyond humanity and any possible celebration of it, I wondered—to the extent that there was any wonder left in me—at my temporary place in the world, wondered how many other countries there were, how many town squares filled with living, with people loving each other, how many windows worth looking through…how many miles it would take to travel farther from or closer to anything that looked even a little like home.

I passed out there, my head on the wooden table, as lost as any man can be.

I took the last of my money and bought an airplane ticket back to Los Angeles. During the twelve-hour flight I passed out so deeply that I had to be shaken awake after we landed, the plane already empty. An attendant under each arm, I was ushered off, down a narrow hallway and into a small room, away from the other people in the terminal. Apparently I was supposed to wait there, for authorities to arrive, perhaps, but as soon as I could get my feet under me, I opened the unlocked door and walked unchecked through and out of the airport. I slowly became aware of—though not particularly bothered by—the fact that at some point during the flight I had peed in my pants.

I tried to stay in L.A., but could not. I felt done there, completely, and didn't want to spend another hour anywhere near it. There were scarce few people I could call for help anymore. Borrowing money one last time, I bought one more ticket.

I went to Memphis, where a few friends still lived. It worked for a while. People who had known me all those years ago now found the tales of my adventures entertaining, in a sordid sort of way. There were spare bedrooms in which I could pass out, spare change I could borrow, kind hearts I could take advantage of. Most would have little to do with my life by then, though, and in their faces I saw a look that said—*Go on, do it, for heaven's sake. If you want so badly to kill yourself, get on with it.* A very few people still loved me, I think. They saw that my dying was not all my own doing, those who really knew me, and it saddened them, though none of them had the experience to help. And so this went on for a while, but eventually even these friends could take no more of me, and finally I drank myself out of virtually everyone's lives.

I had tried to stop. The only thing more terrifying than intentionally trying to kill yourself with drink and drugs is that hopeless, helpless moment when you come face to face with the true demon of addiction, that fear-frozen instant of realization when after an endless stream of days and nights you cry out to the useless gods surrounding you and beg them to help you quit, *but still you can't.* This is a road not on any map of the non-addicted mind, a land of fear and panic and the utter hopelessness of life without faith. This is where we live, lifelessly—embracing the unique misery that comes from the overpowering compulsion to continue the torture, even as the sound of our own screams for mercy bounce off the walls and ring down the hall.

By now, existence was nothing more than a waiting, a resignation. Thirty-four years old, a young man grown
strangely old, done with life and living. Here, really, the
story should have ended. But something else happened.

Another night. There was nothing different about
this one. I wasn't in jail, or lying in the twisted wreckage
of a car. Nothing had occurred to create any sort of environment for self-examination, much less conversion; I
was incoherent, past saving, incapable of accessing my
heart, if I had one left. Nothing now but waiting, waiting,
just one more shapeless night, one of what seemed like
millions all linked together by shadow and emptiness,
passing out, passing away, down once more into nothingness...maybe this time will be it, maybe this time it will
end...drifting off again into blackness, into the things we
remember, into what had once been God-Dreams...

*When I was a little boy I had a rope swing, hung
from the branch of a giant oak tree. One day I flew too
fast or too high or too recklessly, and I fell...*

Then. Instead of death, Life. Instead of prison,
Freedom. Instead of finally succeeding in going to sleep one
night and never waking, of killing or being killed or succumbing to the inevitable overdose, something happened.

*And I prayed—"Oh God, please save me!"—a shout
from my soul that God couldn't help hearing...*

Suddenly, in the silent hours before dawn with the
world perfectly still, I sat up wide-awake, stone sober, as
if I had never slept at all. And on this night, in the unfur-
nished back room of someone's house, lying on an old

mattress on the floor surrounded by unpacked boxes, *something changed*. My memory of the experience begins and ends with this: Startled, eyes wide open in the blackness, instinctively listening. I could not remember having heard anything, or recall any fragment of dream that might have shaken me out of my stupor. Yet I was certain of some disturbance, of something ominous in the silence pressing in on me. The room felt very cold. And as my ears strained against the dark, I became aware of a presence in the room, and somewhere within me and before I could really react I realized that it hadn't been a sound which had brought me back to my senses, but a *Force...*

I felt myself being crushed. The truth of death slammed into me like a train, and I burst into wrenching, agonizing sobs, as if my soul were being torn from my chest, as if there was blood in my tears. On my knees, curled over the mattress like a broken bird, my face pressed into the sheets by a weight threatening to smother me, the futility and longing and utter despair of my life weighing down on me until the breath was forced from my body...*a little boy drowning...*the lost opportunities, the waste of my gifts, the soul-deep hunger for love, for a wife, for children, for the child within me...*I think he's waiting for a friend...*the rush of tastes and smells, spring honeysuckle and gardens and collies, pencils and chalk, grass and soil and lost turtles and rain and Jergen's lotion and clean quilts...*our lips are just about to touch...*winter and fireplaces and pipe tobacco and cedar Christmas trees, crickets and creeks, lightning bugs and bread-and-butter pickles and go-karts, the reason for being, the times of purpose and joy and meaning and belonging...*a mother's hand, God's hand*...a mouth full of dirt and a yellow rope swinging just out of reach, a time of being aware of life and not fearing it, of being on a lost dirt road and knowing somehow we weren't lost at all.

Remember I'm always praying for you.

And the tears began pouring out of me like rain, like hard, deep, crystal cleansing rain until I could not breathe at all, could not see or hear or move, until whatever had been haunting me came rushing out with a shudder and a gasp and helpless hollow howling, and then died.

The room became perfectly quiet. And for the first time in many years, without moving from the spot, I floated effortlessly into the pure and perfect dreams of a child.

Running, running fast. To somewhere very far away and yet very present, a long-closed place within that lay deeper than the wounds, a cool and breeze-blown land by still waters, the lush green grass making whispering sounds, a sweet-silent hillside resting in the shadow of enormous unseen wings—*effortless, three steps, arms spread, I would rise up on the wind*—free, yet owned, lifted, possessed, suddenly weightless, the burden removed, carried beyond the pain, beyond the madness, to a place beyond remembering.

I would fly away and be at rest.

Looking up.

Waking, I did not move. I lay there, blinking dumbly at the light shining through the window as if I had not seen such a thing in a very long time. For the briefest of moments I wondered if perhaps I'd finally succeeded in killing myself. Then, slowly, I began to feel that just the opposite was true. I could no more put it into words now than I could have then, but somehow—in a way that had much more to do with my heart than with my brain—I knew. I understood.

I'm right here.

I heard, felt it. The same companion who had talked me through so many dark nights.

I've been here all along.

The Best Friend who had picked me up out of the gravel and the blood and brushed the dirt from my hair.

You're safe now.

And though it seemed to me as if many lifetimes had passed since I last called out His name, I suddenly realized something that again brought tears from a place not yet dry: *He had not changed.* Time meant nothing to Him. Lying there in His arms, in the afterglow of resurrection, I knew that in His eyes I was again a little boy, once more a child.

His child.

❧❧

When Jesus saw him lying there, and
knew that he had already been a long
time in that condition, He said to him,
"Do you wish to get well?"

—*JOHN 5:6*

In the movies, the script might have had me leaping from the mattress and immediately running through the streets proclaiming the Gospel. But in real life, in my real life, anyway, the way to wellness would be in many ways as long and perilous as the one to ruin. So deep ran the sickness in my spirit and body that much of what transpired the next few days following that one night remains clouded in my memory. Probably I walked around in a sort of stupor for a while; those who happened to cross my path might have suspected that the shattering of what was left of my sanity had finally come, because it isn't likely I could have put together a coherent sentence. I know that I often considered taking a drink—because I no longer knew how to go through a day without doing so—but that somehow I did not. The flash of feeling that had been the face of Christ faded into the mists of my exhausted mind, so that even though I felt changed, I was too weak to understand what it meant, or what step I should take next.

Still, I had surrendered. On some primitive and very human level, I had given up, and given in. I had been given one bright and blinding moment to choose, and by His Grace I had chosen the road to *life*. And from that instant, some strength from both beyond and within seemed to take over, and do for me what I could not do for myself. I was fully aware that I could not save myself, that left alone now I would surely die. Yet, *somehow I knew*. Until the smoke cleared and I could see, He would lead me. Until I was able to take another step on my own,

to find my way to others—the ones He had already pre-
pared and would soon place in my path to help hold me
up—He would lift me. I was far too confused at the time
to rationally think any of this, of course, to reason such
an unreasonable thing. But at last I had fallen back into
the arms of His Grace, and His Grace would prove suffi-
cient. I actually went one day, then another, without
drinking. With me now again His willing and obedient
child, the miracle had begun.

The things we remember.

God only knows how it came to be. I have no idea
how many days had passed. But on one cold and rainy
afternoon I somehow found my way to the downtown
mission, to a meeting in the basement of an old stone
church. I don't remember much about that first visit, or
even exactly how I got there. But one moment will remain
in my mind as long as I live—my hands shaking badly as
I tried to pour a cup of coffee, the stuff spilling all over the
table, and a withered hand reaching in to gently steady
the cup and pour it full. And I remember those eyes, the
eyes of this seventy-three year old woman, and I saw
peace in them.

"Looks like you could use some help," she said.

flying

"My name is Carter, and I'm an alcoholic." His was just another voice in the circle, twenty or thirty of us, there in the damp basement of the mission, seeking refuge from the cold sleet pelting the windows.

"I'm thankful to be here today, thankful to be alive"— a lot of the same words, but there was a sound to his voice, intelligence without pride, humbled and calm and peaceful. "I'm truly grateful for this room, and for you people. With the help of my loving and forgiving God, and the support of each and every one of you, I'm trying to stay clean and sober. And I'm trying to live real life..."

I sat there, shaking, listening, watching his face. *Trying to live real life.* After only a few weeks in, I'd been hammered about the necessity of finding someone with a lot of sobriety to act as a guide, a mentor, a person to share your hidden hurt with, someone who could walk with you through the healing, to help you finally let go of the poisonous secrets. It was all too frightening for me, though. And so I had stayed to myself, mostly, rarely talking during the meetings, knowing I would die if I left these rooms, but not quite willing to surrender fully to them, either. There were days and nights when I thought I couldn't take one more stupid sobriety slogan. They drove me nuts with their simple-sounding sayings and their passive, knowing nods. It was infuriating at times. My anger boiled, the very blood in my veins screaming out for a drink. And again, the nods, and all they would say to me was: "Keep coming back." I wanted to choke them to death with my bare hands.

Still, something kept me there. A little at a time, I began to understand what the people in these meetings were saying. I found their laughter fascinating. Eventually, I began to laugh, too; not the old, too loud, scare-away-the-demons kind of laugh, but a real one from deep down, as if for once in my life I could comprehend the joke. And, maybe more than anything else, I came to admire their courage. On the surface, they looked completely unrelated—homeless people, junkies, lawyers and housewives, pimps and three-piece suit executives—and yet each of them had something glowing in their eyes, something I had never owned and always desired. Courage. And hope. These people had hope. And they had learned through experience that the only way any of us is ever able to hold on to that gift of courage and hope is by giving it away, by sharing it. They had looked Death straight in the eye, and Death had blinked. They were then—and continue to be now—the bravest people I have ever known.

"Anyway," he's saying, "with God's help and the help of you people, I have a chance at life again. Now I go to sleep at night instead of passing out, and I wake up in the morning rather than coming to. I don't have to live like that any-more"—and I thought, just for an instant, that he looked across the room straight at me—"I don't have to be alone."

After the meeting I sat frozen in fear, the palms of my hands wet. I had tried before, rehearsed what I might say, only to sit and watch him walk away without ever leaving my chair. But this time—A deep breath. *What are you so afraid of? Stand up, go, stick out your miserable, sweaty hand. For once, do something brave. Take a chance...*

I had no place to live. Too broke or insane or just plain stupid at the time, I for whatever reasons did not consider checking myself in to a treatment center; I'm not sure that I even knew such places existed. But someone in the fellowship just *happened* to know a friend who would be traveling on business for a couple of months, and, miraculously, I suddenly had a downtown apartment, all to

238 PRODIGAL SONG: A MEMOIR

myself. Looking back, I realize how dangerous this method of self-detox might have been. But a divine hand apparently hovered near.

Other than my meetings, I became a hermit. The first weeks were brutal. The physical reactions to life without booze transformed me into something truly bizarre. Thankfully, few ever saw me. My face turned red, then began scaling and peeling. My weight, which had ballooned out of control during the last few years of my drinking, began to drop dramatically, and my appetite almost disappeared. I spent the days in a borrowed bathrobe, unshaven, hands shaking, trying to eat, then throwing up. I would stare into the mirror for what felt like hours, feeling like Jeff Goldblum in "The Fly," fully expecting parts of my face to begin falling off.

My face, for the most part, did not fall off. But, gradually, other layers were removed, like the slow and painful peeling away of Lazarus' grave clothes, and a little bit of daylight began to reach my eyes. A full year would pass before much more than physical recovery could take place, but in time my pride, my self-centeredness, my loneliness, and the other masks I had worn for so long began to gradually melt away. Unless you've been bound and dead to darkness, it's something difficult to imagine. But the journey back to myself had begun.

❧❦

"Twenty-one years," he says again. I hadn't believed him the first time. He's giving me a ride to a meeting, just as he had for weeks now. The neon night of Memphis moves past us in blurred streaks.

Twenty-one years—I let the words ride out of my chest on a deep, hopeless sigh, feeling small and inconsequential, like an ant surveying the pyramids.

He smiles. "I wouldn't get too hung up on time," he says, one hand on the wheel. In his fifties, face deep-lined, eyes tired and wise, body still military-trim, gray hair cropped close to his head. He looks confident, at ease with himself and with me.

"How the hell did you do it?" I ask, and there must be something miserable in my voice, something straining pitifully against the seemingly endless and impossible road before me, because he looks over for a moment, silent, then back at the road.

"Don't push," he says, and the lightness in his voice is gone. A brief nothing. Then—"Really, all you have to know right now is this:"—And I hold my breath, waiting for the magic solution, the answer to my growing madness, some easy way out. And he says, with the smallest of smiles playing at the corners of his mouth, looking at me as if he's known me all my life—

"There is a God. And you're not Him."

At first the process seemed so slow that I concluded nothing at all was happening. I laughed and cried until my gut ached as much as my heart. I hit my knees every morning and asked for His help. I sat alone for endless hours in a perfectly cool apartment, sweating like a pig. Sleeping seemed impossible; I counted every conceivable kind of animal, including sheep, but always ended up pacing around in the middle of the night, too tired to exercise, too anxious to be still. I didn't have the concentration to watch TV, much less read. I would discover someone's voice in the room, and then realize it was my own, blathering. More than once I caught myself sitting very still in the room, lights turned off, slowly but firmly rubbing the tips of my fingers through my hair, back and forth, something vaguely familiar and soothing about the warm friction against my scalp...and always with this feeling of desperation, of needing to run, of itching to get out of town, out of this madness, out of my skin. Always this feeling of fear.

I learned to ask for help. Without it, I would not have survived. I stayed close to those who were, if not completely free from fear, at least no longer at its mercy. Eventually, becoming desperate enough, I would actually do the daily things they suggested. It helped, though often there seemed to be little rhyme or reason to it.

And I learned to share, maybe the hardest lesson of all. I began to find a kind of solace in the telling of my secrets, a cleansing in my confessions. No one judged me. No one stopped talking to me, or trying to help me. Over time, I began to feel something. I couldn't quite put a word on it at first, still too crazy to understand. And so I just kept coming back to those rooms, to the smoke and the noise and the laughter. Listening, and hoping.

To be part of. To belong.

❧❧

"What are you so afraid of," he asked, gently. I'm beginning to trust him by now, to trust myself, at least a little. I'd always thought of fear as something outside his experience, this former fighter pilot in Vietnam.

"Nothing, really," I lied, and his look shot me down almost at once, and both of us smiled. "Everything," I said, taking a breath. "I'm afraid of everything. Of people. Of getting out of bed some mornings. Of being in the world…" Hesitating, staring at my hands.

After some silence, he finished my thought for me: "Of living," he said. And then in a voice of simplest grace, of utter human intimacy, of anointed absolution—

"Me too."

❧❧

Who knows but the world may end tonight?
—*ROBERT BROWNING*

There were times when I couldn't be with anyone, times when like it or not I had to sit in a room with my own wretched self and no one else. Times when I was hanging on by the thinnest of threads, wanting one, just one drink, *some relief, dammit, for mercy's sake and the sake of my soul just one damn drink, warm and smooth, going down like sweet syrup*…wondering which was worse—the dull, aching prison of my disease, or the open-eyed nightmare of not getting a fix. Half-crazed from the cravings, I cursed myself and God and the world and everything in it, cursed my shaking hands and pounding head and clanging nerves. And the insanity I had feared all my life dared me to die, there in the lost hours, hanging motionless over me like a noose.

And then one night, after being in and out of bed a dozen times, I felt it coming again. I stumbled to the sink, and threw cold water on my face, knowing it wouldn't work. I sensed that foul horror closing in on me, rushing up out of nowhere, threatening to swallow me whole, and the madness flashing in, *a drink, just one drink,* four in the morning, the still silence pressing in on me, my prayers echoing off the walls, *Oh God, here it comes, please make it stop,* but it wouldn't stop, *He's not listening,* the old madness rushing back, out of the walls, blackness, death, *Oh, God, please help me…*

And I'm on my knees, pushing the top of head across the rug, the heat coming through my skull, *oh no, no, God no,* then leaping to my feet, covering my ears, *no, please no, NO!* And my mind is darting, like a cornered animal, looking for a way out, any way out…

*And I was running, running fast…*out into the night, running as if chasing something, as if something were chasing me, out into the black summer night dressed only in gym shorts, the sound of my bare feet hitting the sidewalk a million miles away—*Oh God, sweet Jesus*—my panic pressed back down into my lungs, gasping, choking, the screams muffled, the tears coming and the world blurring, my feet flying through the concrete woods, searching for something familiar but unseen, towards or away from cedars with moss-covered roots and the hope of home hidden in their shade, a turtle in my hand, *please be there, oh God please be there, I'm bringing him home,* my heart bursting, the air thick and sticky-sweet and burning like tender fire through every muscle, and the pain is *good*, scorching up my legs and tearing at my side, connecting me to something, beating back the monster, the fire in my chest roaring against the horror in my head—*leave me* ALONE!—faster, rounding a corner, past sleeping houses, blessed souls at rest, *save me*, fainting, falling, back up, with a merciful tingling in my scraped palms, *I'm still alive*, running, running as fast as I can, from myself, back into myself—WHERE ARE YOU, GOD?— a groaning from within, because I can't get away, can't run fast enough, it's all around me and through me and in me, my feet mired and heavy, like running through blood, pushing, pushing, going nowhere...*a wasp, beating itself to death against the window, tap, tap, tap...*

And then, like hitting a wall, I stop.

Bent over, holding my side, agony rattling in and out of me. At the edge of a curb somewhere, teetering, staring across a great, aching abyss, dazed, looking into a mirage, an oasis, shaking the sweat out of my eyes, trying desperately to focus on this out-of-nowhere white glow, these warm and welcoming fluorescent lights of life, of possible peace, of something still moving in the still dead of night.

The 24-hour market.

I stood there, hypnotized. I didn't know where I was, exactly. But in the dark stood a shining hope, waiting patiently like an old friend. I slowly stood up as straight as possible, gasping for air. Looking through the great glass wall, I blinked blindly at the glimmering colors, hanging there on my concrete ledge, seemingly for hours, for endless nights, barely balanced between seduction and salvation.

And in this moment something else happened—a changing, the soft answering of a shouted prayer, perhaps, some graceful and thoughtless thing beyond myself. I licked my lips and closed my eyes, and opened them again. And the store was still there, and the pain, too. But this time I could see myself, all of me, and felt returned to my own body, as if I'd finally caught up with myself at last, as if the past and the present had suddenly come face to face near the edge of deep woods, at the end of some eternal, circular journey.

And then, I thought I heard something...

We're up very early one morning, just the two of us. Sitting on the porch, staring out into that not-dark, not-light time, the suspended moments before dawn...this sweet stillness, this pause, this holy space between when the crickets stop their music and the birds begin their own, as if God were taking a deep breath...

Time ceased. I looked down at my feet, fascinated, watching the slow-motion drops of blood fall from my nose and trickle between my toes. My legs, shaking. Bare chest shining, the pounding of my heart lifting and falling beneath the skin. A connection. Clarity. A choice, made for me.

"Listen," she whispers.

Always running. Into the night, or away from it. Standing on the edge, wondering what freedom felt like.

And all the earth and sky hung under and over me there, a faint light stirring, in the quiet moments before dawn…
    And I hear the silence. The deafening anticipation. Nothingness. Waiting. As if for some command. Somewhere between remembering and forgetting. Here, now, listening breathlessly for the heartbeat of creation. Just before the birds start singing…
    Turn.
    One, two, several.
    Take a step.
    Then a chorus, sweeping out of the trees.
    Take…one…step.
    I did. Then another.
    Run!
    A deep breath…
    And I'm running, running fast, away, like lightning, terrified and fearless, at first because I could feel the breath of something at my heels, but then, realizing who it was, a second wind—*There You Are!*—New lungs, and lightness, and it's all downhill, the air cooler, my stride swift and clean, suddenly shooting through the streets with my soul on fire, a boy and a dog and the moss like springs beneath my feet, headed somewhere safe, *oh sweet Jesus, sweet Jesus,* and some kind of loony laughter coming up and out of me, the panic falling away like shattered glass, and all at once I'm leaping, shouting, crying for joy, the squirrels scampering up trees, dogs dodging off the walk and out of my way—Look at me! LOOK AT ME!
    A home run, hit left-handed.

Confirmed. Liberated. At long last rounding the bases, eyes closed, nearing home, far from healed but oh so far from dying, the night air roaring past my ears like the sound of a cheering crowd. And I raise my arms with a foreign feeling of *victory*, then spread them out like wings...alive, flowing, soaring into the coming morning on the soft white wings of a dove.

learning

"The more I learn, the less I know," he says. The two of us are walking in the park, along a lake's edge. Nine months now, and not a drop, a joint, or a pill. The impossible is happening. Much more time will have to pass before I have any consistent clarity. But I am beginning to see again, to hear and breathe in things, to appreciate the life, the gift. The cravings ease. I sleep better, and some health returns. I begin to ask questions. I start to wonder.

He and I are friends now, and I'm not afraid of him anymore. We inhabit space together without feeling the need to fill it up with the noise of our voices. He shares with me, as if I were his long-lost brother. Just as someone else had done long ago, he is teaching me to be still. And now he's saying something like, "I don't try too hard these days to figure out God," because he knows I've been doing just that, and that it's making me uneasy. His voice is as soft and calm as the blue-white clouds above us. We walk for a while in silence, then stop and lob stones into the silver water.

Then he says, "All I know is this: There is nothing we can do"—He looked at me, and paused. Then, solid and sure—"Nothing we can ever do that will make Him stop loving us."

And then a feeling, both pitiful and profound, heart-breakingly beautiful. And the words come out of my mouth, without me really having to think them.

"We can always come home."

He looks over at me, a small smile coming.

"Something my grandmother once told me," I say.

He nods, and throws one more stone.

"Yes," he says, satisfied. "We can always come home."

In the deepest and truest sense of who and what we are, we are seemingly always running away from or towards God; either lost or found, turning our backs or reaching out our hands, running away or coming home. Even when we don't believe ourselves to be thinking of Him at all, we are from our very first breaths falling in or out of love with our Savior, this One who has created us and through His presence alone finally completes us. This is how we are made. God, *in us*.

And so I learned how to pray, again, though as it turned out I had never really forgotten. I only needed guidance, a little help back down to my knees, a re-opening of a fully broken heart now willing to ask for forgiveness. I remembered how to ask Him to protect me, to calm the storm outside my window, and the one within. I remembered how to talk with Him, and once past my fear it wasn't difficult at all. I asked Him to be my friend again. And He said *Yes*.

Time passed, and my eyes healed, and the blue seeped slowly back into the sky.

Still without a car, I did a lot of walking. For years my world had moved past me as little more than a colorless blur. But my new eyes could now stare at a simple patch of grass and see each blade, each tiny wildflower. My sneakers were so worn out they barely held together, but still I walked, filling my newborn senses. Some days I strolled for hours, in unknown directions, sometimes getting lost on purpose, I think. And on one very splendid Sunday morning, the sun warm and reassuring, I found myself lost like that, and it felt wonderful. I can't remember the name of the street, or into what part of Memphis I'd wandered, but at some point I heard singing. Sweet voices floated down on me, beckoning, leading me around a corner, and out of the stained glass windows up ahead I heard joy bursting forth and rising up to the sky.

There was not the slightest hesitation. It seemed a very natural and reasonable thing that I should turn off the sidewalk and up the steps. I pushed against the heavy wooden doors, and walked into the simple sanctuary full of people, most of them black, worshipping and praying and making music. Several of them turned as I entered, and motioned me to come on in. No one was sitting. A bunch of folks shuffled down and made room for me at the end of the pew.

Singing. Some of the words I could understand, and some I could not, and, of course, it didn't matter. Part hymnal and part inspiration, yelling and crying, a mystical language all its own, intimate, as if coming through a feather pillow beneath my head—*Na na na, na-na-na-na.* And this divine gift of song caused a stirring in me, and a breaking, my throat tightening until I could make no sound, and so I just stood there helplessly in the heavy wake of its joy.

When the passion temporarily wearied, and the people finally sat, the preacher began shouting and pleading and quoting scripture, most of it rolling over me like indistinguishable but precious babbling. Then, out of all the moaning and thrashing, I heard this, plain as Light:

"And he got up and came to his father.
But while he was still a long way off,
his father saw him,

and felt compassion for him,
and ran and embraced him,
and kissed him…"

And on it went, though I heard no more of it. Because, just as predicted, the Light came back to me. Thirsting for Love, I finally wandered to the edge and half-fell, half-jumped—*drowning*—turned upside down like a lonely little boy in a ditch full of rushing, muddy water. And the healing river ran deep and fast, and I could feel the life I had been desperately clinging to being held under, passing away, gently dying, once and forever. I did not struggle, and stopped trying to float, letting the water take me… *listening for the internal roar of my own breathing, in and out, and the pulse of blood through my body, echoing like a heartbeat in the womb…*

Then I knew: I saw something, hovering above the surface. And I reached for my Father's hand.

And there were warm, healing hands all over me then, on my head, my shoulders, my back. *Connection.* The shameless tears came clean and easy—all the philosophy and psychoanalysis, ego and existentialism, the longing and loneliness and narcissistic nonsense—all of it, washing warm and wondrously out of me, on tears of grace I did not bother wiping away.

Once I had found Him, I felt drawn to find the others. To tell them I was sorry. To tell them that I loved them, even if they could no longer love me. To let them know that I was trying to live real life again, and couldn't really hope to fully do that without first looking them in the eye and telling them the truth.

The people I longed to talk with the most, though, had gone. In this desperate desire for closure I put myself most deeply in His need, and began to draw closer to His Grace. In my yearning to touch my lost loved ones, I cried out to them—as well as to God—in my prayers. Again and again God broke me, and while kneeling my heart would overflow with grief and joy, loneliness and comfort, and a deep sense of His presence. Gradually, week after week, month after month, the poison of remorse and guilt and shame came pouring out with my tears, until finally I would lie exhausted and limp, unable to speak or even think, with nothing but the sure and weightless sense of being held in Someone's arms.

Here, in the safety of this embrace, I listened. And I came to believe, slowly, that hidden somewhere between the dreaming and the waking there waits an indomitable Truth, and within that Truth lives all mystery and meaning, all purpose and plan...for the things we remember, and the things we forget.

When I had been clean for about a year, my heart told me it was time. An irresistible voice called me to my hometown, to those who had known me as a child, and who now—amazingly—would look into my eyes and recognize the child I had once more become. To my sisters, who had loved me through it all, unconditionally, even after I had run away and left them in that place to fend for themselves. They were suffering, too, in their own ways, and our healing would take all of what was left of our lives. We had existed without truly communicating, without in many ways knowing one another. Together, we still had much to discover. We would learn how to mourn, to grieve, to feel. Sharing would come neither quickly nor easily. But now, perhaps, we might begin. At least we could begin.

Home. To my father, who I finally saw as someone who had done his best to protect his children from pain, a husband and dad who had loved us with all of his broken heart, and had tried to shield us in the only way he knew how. Over time, he and I would slowly forgive each other's mistakes, silently acknowledging our separate abandonment, putting away the unspoken resentments and allowing one another to be human, to be broken, to say that we loved each other, and in some wordless way to become father and son once more. I could look up to him again, and see him as a sort of flawed hero, wounded and far from perfect—like me, like all of us—but my hero just the same. Like Captain America.

Home. Back to the places where I played in the woods with my dog and once knew what snow tasted like and what blue sky felt like, returned to that place where the very air was made up of pure, crackling electricity that would rush into my lungs as I ran and shoot out of my sneakers when my flat feet hit the ground...running, silent as stars and shadow, through woods thick with cedar and pine and oak, redbud and forsythia shooting up from the earth like wildfire, dogwood blossom petals floating down like snowflakes behind the house where I used to live…unchanged, mysterious places waiting for other enchanted children to come darting through like bumble bees, like gazelles. To the big hill behind our old house where in summer my sisters and I had rolled down through the tall brown weeds for the sheer joy of rolling, the grasshoppers screaming and shooting out around us in all directions like coiled springs as we giants came rumbling through their secret world.

And then—though it would take many more trips back to my little town before I could summon the courage—to the little white house where Mamaw had once lived and cooked and sung to me, driving slowly by several times, feeling foolish, trying to gather my nerve. I made a final pass, one last, futile attempt, cursing my cowardice, wondering why it was so difficult, why I felt so afraid. But this time, I caught a glimpse of an old man on the porch, the rocking chair pulled over near the screen door to catch more sun. I could see the side of his face, his arms folded in his lap, feet stretched out in the warmth. And something flowed over me, a feeling stronger than my fear, and almost as if I no longer held the steering wheel, the car pulled into the gravel driveway.

Walking toward the porch, I felt myself shrinking with each step, growing shorter and skinnier, barely able to lift my feet from the ground, as if shuffling along under the weight of an oversized baseball uniform sagging from my shoulders. I wanted very much to turn and run. Feeling small and afraid, I silently asked God to help me lift my hand. Taking a deep breath, I gently knocked on the screen door.

"Come in, young man," he said, casually turning his head, almost as though he had been expecting me. He opened the door without hesitation, and it made a very old, very familiar creaking sound.

The moment I set foot on the porch, I felt immature, tongue-tied and flat-footed, stepping back into another time. My heart raced. And yet he would treat me like a long lost son, getting me a glass of water, listening quietly as I stuttered of my past in the house, my grandparents, my youth. He never blinked, not seeming in the least surprised by my visit, or my history. He invited me to pull up a chair, and we talked for a while. Small and gentle, an old brown sweater buttoned at his withered neck, he spoke of living alone in the house for the past several years. He seemed very much at peace with my presence, never questioning my motives, this old fellow who had heard of my grandparents but never met them.

While he stayed sunning on the porch, I walked through the once-enchanted kitchen barely the size of a closet, and the tiny back bedroom where we had slept, where Papaw's old desk once sat in the corner with a drawer full of horehound candy and pocket knives and the musty-sweet smell of *time*...through the back yard where a garden once grew, now long abandoned and surrendered to the grass and weeds, where long ago I sat in the warm dirt eating fresh cherry tomatoes and leaf lettuce while Papaw planted corn.

Later, the short autumn day giving way to evening, the two of us sat there together on that same screened porch which once had seemed so vast and now felt so small, this magical place where I spent so many full and filling days, and where now all these years later, the sun slipping again behind some very old and familiar trees, he and I spoke of my life and of his, and of the framed picture I had noticed hanging on the wall of what was now his bedroom—the photograph of a handsome young military man, his own lost son.

"I miss him, of course," the old man said. "And I miss my wife, too." He rocked gently, the toes of one foot on the floor, well practiced, rhythmic. "We had a real nice place back then, the house where our boy was born." A faint smile played across his lips, as if he were looking at something very beautiful, or an old photograph, perhaps. "After we lost Mack…well, things never quite got back to being right again. Margie never really got over it. Her heart stayed broken until the day she passed."

There was silence for about a minute, nothing but the steady squeaking of his chair.

"This place suits me fine, though," he said finally, gently. "It's my home now, and I like it here." He paused, and we listened to a bird sing. A cardinal, I think.

"And in a way," he said after a moment, "it's your home, too."

Many months later, after repeatedly driving past the old cemetery, unable to stop, the same way I had once long ago hurried past her doorway as she sat staring into the storm, I finally gave up trying to find the strength on my own. Surrendering, I let my Friend gently take my hand and lead me white-faced and shivering to my mother's graveside, where kneeling in the cold mist I prayed for her soul, and for mine, and cried out to her and to Him for forgiveness, my rehearsed words falling uselessly away with the tears...*I'm so sorry, so sorry, Momma.* And there on my knees in the wet brown grass, the wind blowing all the way through me, I received a gift that forever broke and healed my heart.

I saw her lips, red as apples...eyes like sparklers...with dancing shoes on her feet. And, coming from a place much deeper down than where things usually come from...

I saw her soul smile.

Three years clean and sober. I was beginning to understand.

I had never known how to love. So that, even when I'd given up drinking and drugs, I kept using other things. Some still-unsatisfied part of me continued to seek solace from others, from the warmth of their company, the false intimacy of their closeness. Still selfishly seeking something from them—wholeness, meaning, a balm for the part of me not yet complete. And, for a short while, I went right on with this behavior, using people almost out of habit, simply substituting my drug of choice, opting for this easy medication rather than diving full force into the healing.

Soon, though, after being sober long enough to clear away at least some of the debris in my heart, this stopped working altogether. The emptiness would not be filled. I began to realize on yet another level that nothing from the outside was going to fix me on the inside. And what had once seemed like very natural behavior now began to repel me, to cause a twisting turmoil in my spirit. For a while, I went through the motions; it was the only thing I knew, the only kind of affection I felt worthy of. But I was beginning to know that something was wrong. These were *people*—living people, with hopes and fears and beating hearts, children trying to survive, searching for something, yearning for more than mere physical connection. They were real. They belonged to Him. They deserved more.

I stopped trying to fill myself with someone else. I moved to Nashville to be nearer my hometown, got a job, rented an apartment. Like some poor thirty-five year old just turned eighteen, I awkwardly relearned how to pay my bills, clean my bathroom, and slowly become responsible.

I began writing songs again. For the longest time, I couldn't get near a piano; seeing one, I would walk the other way, as if hurrying from someone I didn't want to talk to. But slowly, gently, God began leading me back, reintroducing us, allowing us to reconcile. Our reunion was tentative. The instrument and I approached one another warily. We had to begin again, one finger at a time.

Starting over. I did what kids ten years younger were doing, standing with them in line at the Bluebird Cafe, melting in the summer sun, hoping for a chance to sing one or two songs on Open Mic Mondays. At first, and for a long while, I felt certain I could never again perform in front of an audience. Without a drink, I sat paralyzed, my hands shaking so badly I couldn't play. I was willing, of course, to give it up for the sake of my sobriety. I didn't even feel sure God wanted me back in music at all; it felt dangerous, being back on stage, the center of attention again. But, *not* doing it didn't feel right, either. So I kept trying. And, over time, it got better.

These experiences were both humbling and energizing. My skills were considerably deteriorated. But nobody knew me; they listened, with no reason to judge. They had never seen me as either Rock Star or drunkard, and so they sat there in the darkened clubs, faceless, sometimes unimpressed but always unbiased. I was just another hungry songwriter in a town full of them. A nobody. Small. Vulnerable. Reborn.

Miracles. They really do happen. On our knees each morning, sometimes praying, other times simply trying to still the shouting inside our souls. Resisting temptation. Asking for help. One day. Another. And another. And then, when we least expect it, the miracles show up, a by-God True thing right smack in the middle of another ordinary and unsuspecting day.

It's the way He speaks to us, sometimes. Softly, almost casually, and nearly always when our heads are turned the other way. If we aren't careful, we miss Him. I had gone for years, pretending to be unaware of Him altogether. Now I was trying, again. Trying to listen.

~~~

Falling in love was the last thing on my mind that day. I was growing more independent from alcohol, drugs, relationships, finally going along each day without all the attachments that had separated me from Him. Learning to live real life. Learning to *be* again. A nice, steady pace. Most days, it felt good.

Miracles. After a year in town, I now held a coveted position as staff songwriter, actually making my living writing for a Nashville publisher. I was living the kind of story that isn't supposed to happen, going through the days marveling at His mercy. The gifts were far greater than I deserved. He had given me back my life, and then my career. I hadn't expected either.

And so, she came as a complete surprise. All those years, my life going in one direction and hers in another. So many possible turns, near disasters, last-minute decisions, twists of "fate." All of that—bringing her here, from North Carolina to New York to Nashville, into this office, on this one day, to apply for a job as receptionist. Coming down the stairs and seeing her standing there, long auburn hair falling past her shoulders onto a simple summer dress, I had to stop for a moment. I could barely breathe.

Finally I reach the bottom of the stairs, and she turns, and we are looking right at each other. Her eyes are as blue as the sky. The color of the sky when I was a little boy.

I walk past her desk, and put a small piece of paper next to her hand.

"Call me sometime," I say, casually. She looks up, bemused, silent, not sure if it's a joke.

I walk out of the building, right across the street to a restaurant, pick up the pay phone, and punch in the numbers.

"Collins Music. May I help you?"—her voice.

"What's the matter?" I say. "You haven't called me yet."

It's funny how God asks us to surrender something before He decides we should have it. We offer it up to Him, and become perfectly willing for our possession to be forever taken away. "Here, Lord"—we say, finally—"Take this from me. I've held on to it long enough. I want it. I have always believed I needed to have it to live. Maybe I do. Maybe I'll die without it. If that's what you want, then I'll do it, I'll die. But take it from me, God. It doesn't belong to me now." And then it's gone, out of our hands, and though we hurt for it and miss it for a little while, He holds us close, letting us rest near Him, comforting us, stroking our hair. And in time—if we're faithful, as faithful as children—there comes a sense that He is well pleased. Then, when He thinks we're ready, just when we're quite sure we don't need it anymore, He gives us something back. Something far more precious.

⤳⤲

"Six years was enough," she is saying. "I got on the subway one morning, and just became aware of it, the dirt and the noise, all of it." I watch her as she speaks, thinking how wonderful it would be to look at her forever. "And I just knew I'd had enough. No more waiting tables, auditioning, dreaming of the theatre. I just wanted to be closer to home."

We sit there, side-by-side, talking for hours. A minor league baseball game, though I remember not a moment of it. Her voice, the music of it, and the way it made me feel listening to it, that's what I remember. The sparkle. The splash of freckles across her nose.

And later, walking to the car, her childlike gasp as she suddenly stops, looking up at the sky. "Oh my!" she says, breathlessly, like a little girl, and I knew in a flash I wasn't worthy of her. I look up, too, and see it, the moon huge and low and deepest crimson, the color of rubies, as if it had suddenly caught fire.

"That's for you," I say. "That's our moon."

And it's no line. This time, I believe it. I am telling the truth.

⤳⤲

Healing. He does it in such marvelous ways, ways we could never imagine on our own. Standing there in my tuxedo, with no feeling in my legs. At the front of the church, paralyzed, there in front of friends and family, in her hometown in North Carolina.

I feel as though I'm dying. Concentrating. Trying not to faint. So completely certain, until this very moment. And suddenly, Old Voices:

Swore I'd never marry. Never.

Organ music playing. In a moment, she will come down the aisle, towards me.

Do you love me?

Thirty-seven years old, shaking like a leaf.

Please, please, does anyone love me?

There is no blood moving in me. My hands are ice.

¿Me amas? Necesito que tú me digas estes palabras... You can't love anything, can you?

Here she comes, the music swelling, on her father's arm...

Can I love anything? Sweet Jesus, please tell me now. Can anyone love me?

The sun coming through enormous windows behind her, and she is silhouette, storybook, moving towards me slowly, gliding, knowing the truth about me, what I was, about my past, yet still smiling and confident, believing, somehow sure of me, coming to me all white lace and satin.

Can...I...love...her?

Through space and time, past pain, a new life and chance, here, in this place, beyond countless other days and dreams...

Yes.

And, for one moment, one breath, I close my eyes and listen again, just to be sure.

Yes.

He said *Yes.*

MR and JB—School Pictures 2002
*I'm putting little photographs of my children in my
wallet. My wife has written on the back, marking
the time. Someday, perhaps, a great many summers
and falls and winters and new springs from now,
they will end up with other memories, years and
years of them, all tossed into a big box and left in a
dark basement. And, on those rare nights when
grace glows brightly enough, someone both a part
of us and yet wholly separate will find them, and
turn them over in their hands like time-jewels—like
breadcrumbs, scattered in the moonlight—leading
them to a place of remembering, a place far away
and yet near enough to touch, to taste, to feel. And
they will wonder...*

I stare at them, sometimes. This family, this house. This
Home. This life, risen from the ashes. And it's as though
I'm dreaming God-Dreams again. Ten years together. We
look back on all the steps taken by both of us and see in
them His amazing weaving of things that ultimately
brought us together. Even now, I often catch myself startled by the gift, constantly awed by the unlikely reality of
them in my life. I'll sit still (in one of those rare moments
when it is possible to do so) and watch them, blinking,

astonished. They are so much more than I deserve, and so much more than I'd ever hoped or prayed for, that there can be only one possible explanation for their nearness. When I'm lying in bed with my wife, or sitting with my daughter in the back yard listening to the songbirds — *Which one is it? Cardinal? Mockingbird?* — or holding the latest last hope for the lineage, baby James, in my arms just before he drifts off to sleep, it becomes as clear to me as it is mysterious.

They are miracles.

Learning. I'm still learning how to feel. I have learned a great deal from my wife, and from her family. I envy the way some people cry, for instance. My wife is one of them. She may never know how God has blessed her— blessed to have always been her mother's friend, to have never abandoned her even when she was living in another town. Blessed to have never disappeared from her family into the dark recesses of a soul-less, empty selfishness. When her mother died, Teresa had something more in her heart to help pull her through. Though she misses her mother now, and sometimes mourns for her and longs for the times when they were together, she has peace. She can live her life knowing that their relationship was rich and full, and that whenever they hurt one another they always made up, always said they were sorry. They were able to say good-bye knowing that they never broke each other's heart and left it that way. She can always look back and, remembering, feel the sorrow that comes from missing a great friend; and through those cleansing tears, experience the inexplicable joy of knowing that the friend is never really gone. She can live real life, without regret.

And yet, for some of us, perhaps this is where God steps in. Maybe it's never too late, even for those of us resigned to the loss. If we let Him, He touches us, and guides us to a place where we might find mercy in our memories, and grace in our regrets. This is where Jesus comes alongside and offers us what could be the greatest gift of all—the chance to choose whether we wish to be haunted by our dreams, or healed by them.

Always learning. Changing does not come quickly, or easily. I know for certain that I won't do everything right as a husband, or a parent. I'll make mistakes. And I can't help wondering how my own children will one day see me. Will they forgive my failures? Will I be a hero in their eyes? God knows I'm trying. I've decided, though, to do at least some things a bit differently. I'll start small, maybe letting my kids live a little dangerously—eating the top layer from a new jar of pickles, for instance, or recklessly washing their hair first thing in the shower. Who knows; maybe I'll even let them sit near the window one day, watching a thunderstorm. When they're older, perhaps.

For now, I'm trying to take baby steps. When my little girl comes running to me in tears and in need, I pick her up and I hold her against my chest, both of our hearts beating there together. Something very old and very afraid inside me wants to tell her to be strong, wants to beg her not to cry, because I can't bear to be a part of her pain. I want to insulate her. I want to always make her laugh, knowing that it's impossible. And the truth is, of course, she doesn't really belong to me. But instead of saying don't cry, don't hurt, don't feel, I now try to pray for strength and wisdom. If I wait, and listen, He comes. And then I take a deep breath and repeat to my daughter what He is saying to me: It's okay, Daddy's gotcha, go ahead and let it out, let the tears come. It's okay to feel. I can't keep you from hurting. But, if you'll let me, I can keep you from hurting alone.

It's been over fourteen years now. I have not taken a drink or a drug in all that time. I have, one day at a time, grown young. And so it's through Him that I now try to see myself, and to discover what it is in this world that's of any real value. It's often painful, but as I walk with Him I seem to be slipping back into the well-fitting garment of peaceful, innocent reality He always meant for me to wear. If God is truly transforming me into a new creature, then I now have access to His eyes, and can shut mine for good and forever. Maybe I will one day and to some small degree be finally able to see myself the way He sees me; when that happens, the transformation will be nearly complete. I'll love things worth loving, and avoid as best I can things that are not. I'll once and for all be capable of something that has not been possible for most of my existence: I will appreciate the Gift. I'll finally accept it, without having to understand it, and simply embrace the knowing that life is, in some exquisite and mysterious way, a Gift; and that if it is indeed a thing given to us by Him in love, then all of it must be seen that way—the grief and the joy, the living and dying, our loneliness and longing, our seeking and finding. And I will hold on as tightly as I can to these flawed, imperfect, perfectly precious people He has provided to walk with me through it all.

This would be a wonderful place to say "And They Lived Happily Ever After," and close the book. But I'm learning that faith is a journey, and that mine is far from over. And so, as I attempt to dig deeper into the word of God, the word digs deeper into me, and I begin to realize that each destination is often only a brief resting spot, a place for preparation. The day is always new. If I ever hope to truly learn the difference between mere happiness and His fulfillment, I'm going to have to put my shoes back on, for much new road lies ahead.

We fall. And if we get up, He changes us. Again and again.

❧❧

Without your wounds
where would your power be?
…The very angels themselves
cannot persuade the wretched and
blundering children on earth as can
one human being broken
on the wheels of living.
In Love's service,
only wounded soldiers
can serve.
—THORNTON WILDER

Going through the file. *Rebecca M. Age 34, divorced, 1 child 5yrs. DOC morphine, Loritab, Xanax, HTOC – TXx2—inability to achieve abstinence as evidenced by OD on RX meds...*

Tired. I close my eyes and gently rub them with the tips of my fingers. A deep breath, hold it, blow it out. Opening my eyes, I see through the small office window a perfect day in late October—an open field, several acres of rolling hills and a jagged wedge of cliff cutting into the cloudless blue sky...a wall of far-off trees, orange and burgundy and gold, barely moving in the breeze. I want to go outside and take a walk. But there's one more person to see.

Back to the folder lying open on my desk—*CD related depression aeb PT description of near-fatal car accident due to DUI—severe damage to right leg + head trauma resulting in stroke-like symptoms*—In treatment twice before. Full of anger. Tried to commit suicide by "cheeking" her prescription meds so the nurses couldn't see, saving them, until she finally had enough to swallow all at once. *Somewhat obvious,* I think, *trying to OD right there in a detox ward.*

And then she comes in. Bad limp. Even through her jeans I can tell one leg is terribly twisted. She sits down awkwardly in the cramped little cubicle, across from my desk, her head near the window. She does not look at me.

Hello, Rebecca, I say, somewhat automatically, still a bit new at it all, still feeling under-qualified and unworthy, as if she should be interviewing me.

"My name is Jim," I say, and she has her head turned at an angle, so that I see her dark profile silhouetted against the bright blue beyond. "I just need to ask you some questions. It's really just so we can better help you." My voice sounds flat and lifeless, despite my efforts to appear caring. She is not looking at me. Her whole body is tense, mouth drawn tight.

"Whatever," she says. Her voice is husky, another permanent affect of the accident. It's all in the file: her little girl had been in the car, and miraculously survived without a scratch. Still, she is overwhelmed by guilt, full of shame. One corner of her mouth is turned down, her speech slightly slurred. I can tell she was once very pretty. *She thinks she's ugly*—a voice in my head, and I feel guilty being so lost in myself, so detached. Her hands shake a little, and she tries to keep them still by clenching them in her lap. Her eyes avoid mine.

I ask the questions, questions she by now has answered already—*Have you had any other previous counseling? Are you attending the group meetings? Recent surgeries...medications...primary care doctor...insurance...*She answers in brief, unemotional tones, half-looking out the window. She doesn't want to be here. She doesn't want to be anywhere. I feel foolish.

"Just a few more," I say softly, wearily, turning a page. I look up at her, and clear my throat. "Can you describe any anxiety and/or depression whether associated with chemical use or not, any changes in sleeping/eating patterns...past history of suicidal/homicidal ideation"—she blinks at this, straightening slightly, but still won't look at me.

Finally, she takes a deep breath. "I just want out of this damned place," she says.

And at that moment, without the least warning, something breaks inside me, and I suddenly snap out of it—out of my own lost place, my *self*, and I look up from the papers in front of me and stare at her, *into* her. For a long moment we are silent, and then I say, without really thinking—

"How do you feel?"

And she half-laughs, sarcastically, barely rolling her eyes, as if to spend one more minute with someone this stupid will surely drive her even more mad.

"Oh, I feel just fine," she says, her voice dry as hot sand, and the words are heavy with things I know well, dark and troubled things, hurt and helplessness and a longing to be done with it all, for it to just be finished and over at last. And then she starts to say something more, but stops short, turning her face once more toward the window.

And I watch her for what seems a silent forever. Then my throat tightens, and something rushes up from my heart into my eyes, and I say—

"*Lonely.*"

Her hands pause. She seems to hold her breath. She still does not turn.

"*Lonely,*" I say again, and my voice has all the oppressive fatigue of hopelessness hanging on it still, as if for this one moment we are one, and the world outside the window has lost its color. And though I know it's now a part of my own past, still it comes at me with a very real immediacy, a startling *closeness,* and I'm crushed by the weight she carries, the one each of us carries, aware of its realness, its gloom.

"*You feel lonely,*" I say, softly, closing the folder, abandoning the script, no longer separate from her. And she slightly turns her head—*a door, cracking open*—and looks right at me, into me, as though she suddenly thinks she recognizes an old acquaintance, as if she has just heard the first word spoken in her native language in a great many years...and we see one another clear as day, identical strangers, bound together by some wordless thing, unspoken and undeniable, inseparable...caught hiding in our secret emptiness, staring into the mirror of our faces, an unrelenting reflection of our truest, desperate selves. It is the most fleeting of moments, this wall falling away, her eyes softening and watering, the eyes of someone I have known all my life...

Her eyes. My eyes.

"Love launches me Godward," writes friend and author Timothy Jones. And so goes this process of searching for true love—some days blasting off into a stratosphere of serene faith, other days barely making it off the launch pad. Balance remains elusive, my soul still sometimes precariously poised on a ledge between insanity and sanctuary. More often than not, I don't feel at all sure-footed. But now, by His grace alone, I head out again down a different road, singing a new song. And though for the longest time I dragged my feet and refused to surrender to the apparent illogic of the call, I've now settled more

peacefully into this new role God has created for me, this
role that He has always been waiting for me to step into
and fill, this place where by His unfathomable mercy I
have been led all along. Looking back at the paths I've
traveled, I'm awestruck by the complexity of His pur-
poses. All along. *He knew.*

I'm finally letting go and learning to obey, and the
peace in it—as is often the case with Him—defies con-
ventional wisdom. So I go, anywhere He sends me, working with people just like me, singing my songs and telling
about what has happened in my life, little church or big,
rest home or prison or treatment center, trying to offer
them at least a glimmer of hope in the midst of their hopelessness. Other times I work in a place that feels very
right, a place where I see a lot of tragedy but also sometimes miracles, privileged every so often to witness a bit of
His Healing—a lost soul found, a death sentence lifted,
the re-opening of a morning glory at dawn. I have found
out what I am, and I am trying to *be that.* Like the unseen
birds just before a new day, I now know where the music
comes from. God tells me when to sing.

This time I'll try not to be the one yelling out directions. Amazingly, He lets me drive. But when He says
TURN HERE, I turn—it's the rule of the game. And each
step I take that brings me closer to His Will is nothing less
than a sometimes reluctant, stumbling step towards *Joy.*

I am still an alcoholic. I will always be an addict, forever
tempted by anything that helps me hide from myself and
from God. Most days I can barely remember what my life

was like back then, and what memories remain flash through my mind as if from a badly written movie, starring some half-bit actor pretending to be me. And in those moments I usually feel safely removed from it all, just some mildly amused observer with a bag of popcorn between my legs, chuckling at the funny parts and stealing an embarrassed sideways glance at the rest.

And yet…and yet there are days when, right out of the blue, I feel a tap on my shoulder and turn to see *him*— someone menacing and strangely familiar, with an unshaven face full of fear. And he speaks to me of things no one else could know, secrets so deeply hidden only a sorcerer could have dug down into the pit of me and unearthed them, and he grabs me by my arm right there in the broad light of any given day and whispers things to me. He invites me to places long ago torn down, and makes me feel things still breathing within me that I felt sure had died forever. I hate him, of course. But there are days. There are days when I actually pause to listen, mesmerized, suddenly oblivious to the miracle of new life all around me, heavy-lidded and high on the fumes of his breath. *And I consider going with him.*

Usually, I see him only briefly. He enters and exits my mind so quickly that, in those rare moments when it happens, I sometimes try to pretend he was never near at all. Still, it can be blinding, like a brilliant flash of darkness. Other times, he comes to me in dreams—"drinking dreams" we call them—and I wake weakened and weary, bone-tired and hung over, as if just returned from a very long journey. I have prayed to be free of it, asking time and again to have this thing permanently removed. But, for His reasons, God has chosen to close my open wound over the thorn, leaving it there, so that the bleeding is stopped but a lingering pain remains. It happens less often with the passing of time, as I learn to surrender more and more to Christ, and let Him have me. I am mostly at peace with it now, not as resentful, a bit more willing to accept the reasons He made me as I am, ever hopeful that He can somehow use my broken-ness in ways I may never fully understand.

Sometimes, the people I work with have trouble with the whole "recovering" thing, as if true healing is somehow less miraculous when performed as a process rather than an event. But to me, nothing could be more beautiful or meaningful than a God who is willing to meet me on my knees every morning, and to walk with me one step at a time, this friend Jesus who seeks relationship rather than waving a magic wand.

"For that which I am doing, I do not understand," Paul bravely confessed in his letter to the Romans. "For the good that I wish, I do not do; but I practice the very evil that I do not wish." Sounds to me like someone struggling with being human. And what it says about us as human beings, I think, is that we will by our very nature and for as long as we occupy these mortal bodies have to deal with our wounds, even *after* the blinding, cleansing light of our own Damascus road.

So what does this mean? It means that each day—each *sober* day—is a gift. It means that every morning I must fall to my knees and ask the One who saved me to save me again. This is true for all of us, of course. We're only human, you know—satisfied or hungry, full of joy or full of fear, aching for Jesus or just plain aching.

As for this prodigal son, I came back expecting nothing, begging for my very life. And I found that not only had He been waiting for me to return, but that He had actually come running down the road to meet me halfway—as if to say: *You needn't try to find your way back all alone. You only have to turn in my direction. I'll walk with you the rest of the way.* And the Father embraced and kissed me, placed a robe across my shoulders and a ring on my finger, and returned to me the very Universe.

The hand of Christ, turning lepers into heirs of the Kingdom. It's something none of us in this lifetime will ever be able to quite get our minds around, of course, and can only hope to barely comprehend with our hearts—this One who created with a thought the vast universe, who with one sweep of His hand scattered the stars like weightless dust from one edge of the Heavens to the other—that in some unfathomable way this same Creator of All would, at the simple sound of our crying, respond with such intense intimacy as to *make Himself one of us,* both God and flesh, sharing all the suffering and profound lonliness that comes with being human...*our eyes...His eyes.* Those of us who have been graced by His forgiveness and will now never be the same...and those of us still one life-changing moment away with the sweet sound of His name poised on the tip of our tongues, caught on our breaths...we, all of us, even as we deny Him and curse Him and turn from Him cannot for long deny the very human truth that we so desperately *need* Him.

"Matthew, Mark, Luke, and John,
Hold my horse till I leap on;
Hold him steady, hold him sure,
And I'll get over the misty moor..."

And so we go through our lives, pretending to be okay when we are not, acting as though we know the way when in fact we couldn't be more lost. Though some of us over time become more convincing actors than others, the truth is we are all more or less faking it. But in our secret, silent selves there sits a lonely little child, head tilted, ear turned hopefully toward a distant yet still-familiar voice...

"Follow me."

The words come so quietly, barely a whisper. At first, when we realize who spoke them, we weep tears of thanksgiving. But with the passing of time, sometimes hours, sometimes years, we begin to doubt their source. We spend our lives waiting for something so dramatic, so explosive, and then this gentle, breathless voice passes through us with such calm that, if we choose, we can easily lose it in the chatter and clatter that fills our lives. What was it? *Who* was it? My imagination, my subconscious, the all-too-human voice of my heart? And, of course, we know somewhere deep within the child of us that it is all of these things and yet much more. But if this is really the voice of God, why not more fireworks? So, for a while, we put it off, and when we're not immediately punished for pretending it isn't real, we feel convicted that perhaps it never was.

Still. Still something nags at us, something both tender and crushing, a *feeling* that only by succumbing to whoever or whatever keeps putting the warm breath in our ear can we perhaps ease this vague despair within us. *Follow me. Give up everything. Only I can fill the emptiness within. I am the answer to the hungering question, the unrelenting hopelessness, the heart-haunting sense that there is something more. You have heard my voice. Now nothing else will satisfy.* But I am not worthy. My motives are not yet pure. He hasn't faxed me an itinerary yet. And on and on, putting off the inevitable, until finally the longing becomes greater than the fear, and we follow. To God-Knows-Where.

The Mystery of Faith. Perhaps much of what we strain to see along our walk is meant to remain veiled to us, and so it becomes a simple matter of obedience. By God's Grace I have been saved from my darkness, and freed from the bondage of self. Sometimes it's the lightest touch of His hand on my shoulder, and other times a strength that forces me to my knees, but no matter how far from His house I roam He never gives up on me. *Follow me*, He keeps saying. *Follow me Home.*

And though often we hear only whispers while waiting for the thunder, this much at least seems clear: When in helpless faith we surrender to Him our shattered souls, hell is a prison that cannot hold us.

❧❧

I go back there now. I'm not afraid of it anymore. From a very selfish point of view, I'm glad the Boom never happened; I like the little town just as it is. I take my new family, and we drive the hundred miles to visit the people we love. We eat fried catfish and hush puppies. We cruise by the old school and the house on the hill. We visit the cemetery, and say prayers together. And on lazy afternoons with the wind rustling through the tops of giant oaks, I sit with my father and look out over the river, the blackbirds swirling dark over our heads like a storm, then quickly gone.

Sometimes we go to the First United Methodist Church. Often, they ask me to perform. I sit at the piano and sing my new words telling of my new life, and the changeless sunlight pours through the stained glass windows as if time has been standing still for decades, the mystery of God and His weaving of things there in the comfortable creaking of the pews, ever floating through the place on a song of love unknown.

Only a few people who were close friends of my grandparents are still living. Some of them are very old now, but very much unchanged in my eyes, as perhaps I am in theirs. The men shake my hand, their touch warm and familiar. And the women always hug me, tears in their eyes, pressing their frail bodies against me as if I were still a child, and sometimes they might whisper into my ear, "How proud Mary Jo and your Mamaw must be of you now. How they must be smiling in Heaven."

And holding on to them, my face pressed down into the still-fresh smells of their Sunday dresses...a place of remembering, of time and tears and hand lotion, of a passing winter and the coming of an endless Spring, where secrets can no longer harm us...I know in this deep-down place beyond my broken heart that what they say is forever true. Closing my world-weary eyes, I finally see with childlike grace that those who find themselves lost—lost but not alone—are at long last nearing home.

"It's a Gift, Mamaw...we have to GO!*" And I take her hand and pull her towards the door...outside, into the Rambler...gone, like clouds across blue, like pioneers, like sailors headed fearlessly towards the edge of the earth...*
Like children.

about the author

Jim Robinson is an award-winning songwriter, singer, producer, musician, and speaker. His songs have been recorded by major artists in country, Christian, and rock music, among them John Michael Montgomery, Restless Heart, The Martins, B.J. Thomas, Neal McCoy, Van Zant, Al Denson, Asleep At The Wheel, and many others. He has also recorded CDs of his own— "ProdigalSong" and "Clean," with a third CD project underway. Recently, many of his Praise and Worship compositions have been adapted into major choral arrangements, performed in places of worship worldwide.

A graduate of Christ Center School of Counseling and Addiction Studies, Robinson also works as a professional Recovery Counselor, in private practice with a team of clinical therapists at PowerLife Resources / The Counseling Center in Nashville. Combining music, speaking, and educational workshop presentations, he travels and performs in churches, treatment centers, schools, and correctional facilities throughout the country.

He lives with his wife and two children in Tennessee.

For more information about
ProdigalSong Ministries,
or to order educational materials,
CDs, or books, please visit
www. ProdigalSong.com

acknowledgements

As is often the case when attempting to tell the truth, the truth is we cannot tell it *all*. Editorial considerations, structural concerns, and confidentiality all play a role in what eventually finds its way into—or gets left out of—every story. In my case, I wanted to point out that a number of people who played very important roles in my life (and survival) are, for any number of reasons including those just mentioned, not represented in this book. Should any of you ever happen to read this, you will know who you are, and I want to say Thank You. In particular, a heartfelt embrace of affection for Gary and Kat Brown, who at one critical point in my life truly came to my rescue, and provided a safe place. I will always love you both. And a special hug for Dorothy Smith, who, very early on, taught me that Love comes in all colors.

All my gratitude to: Almighty God, who managed to get this thing written despite my protestations, and to all my faithful family at St. Bartholomew's Church. And to my readers, who gave of their time and their hearts to walk with me through various stages of early manuscripts, always generous with their advice, encouragement, and prayerful insight: Z. Bryan Haislip (a gifted lover of literature who also happens to be my father-in-law, for his ongoing support and inspiration), Joette Bivens, Betty Robinson, Ron Doyle, Owen & Elise Kieffer, Robert White Johnson, Susan Schumacher, Keith Wheatley, Donna Floyd, Pat Bowlby, Patrick Carr, Kay Morss, Ruth Roberson, Amy Johnson, J.D. Stigall, Marcie Beasley, Charles Lively, Nancy Ann Hardee, and Pamela White.

To my dear friend Bill Bowlby, whose affirmation, motivational e-mails, and uncanny insight (not to mention proofreading skills) came to my rescue at a time when fear and uncertainty—the lonely enemies of every writer—were about to make me surrender.

To Mary-Russell Roberson, who graciously shared her ideas, craftsmanship, and kindred writer's heart.

To Mike O'Neil, mentor and brother, one who has taught me much and continues to teach. And to Dianne O'Neil, who brought us all together, and opened up a new world for me; you are both such a blessing in my life. Let's go fishin.' To the Dream Team, for sharing with me their remarkable courage. To Michele DeFilippo, who so patiently shared with me her wonderful gifts of design and production, and to Dawn Rodgers Wyse for her last-minute artistic contributions. And to everyone at SonLight Publishing, especially Michele Hall, Dean O. Master, and S.G. Hopper.

To James W. Robinson, who proved himself a hero indeed by giving his blessing to the publication of this story. Thank you, Dad.

To Timothy Jones—teacher, editor, prayer partner, brother in Christ, gifted author and even more gifted friend; without your generosity of spirit and gentle but firm involvement, this book would probably be little more than a jumble of unhealed hurts still rattling around inside my heart. From the very beginning, it was your encouragement and guidance that gave me the emotional freedom to write this book. Now, I think it's your turn to buy the coffee...

To my children, and perhaps someday grandchildren—I pray one day you might read this story, and in its pages find lessons not focused on the failures of a man, but on the redeeming glory and grace of Christ Jesus.

And to my wife, Teresa—you gave up so much of yourself to allow me the stolen moments to write, to cry, and to heal. Thank you for walking with me through this ever-new childhood.

SonLight Publishing offers a full line of books,
workbooks, audio/video, music, and Christ-centered
Twelve Step recovery resource materials,
including the nationally acclaimed
Power Life series. For more information,
contact us at:

SonLight Publishing
2711 Murfreesboro Road Suite 105
Antioch TN 37013

Phone: 615-361-0052
Fax: 615-361-9264

Book Orders: 615-331-0691

www.powerliferesources.com